RARE STAMPS

Reflections on Living,
Breathing, & Acting

Terence Stamp

With a Foreword
by
Christopher McQuarrie

ESCARGOT BOOKS

Published by

Escargot Books Online Limited
North Yorkshire, England LS21 2JJ

ISBN:
978-1-908191-38-0 (trade paperback)
978-1-908191-05-2 (ePub)
978-1-908191-18-2 (Kindle)

Cover Photograph © Rankin 2011

Author Photograph © Betina La Plante 2012

All other photos are from Terence Stamp's personal collection, production stills from the credited movies, or publicity stills.

Print layout: eBooks By Barb for booknook.biz

For Maude and Calixte

I wish to thank my friend and colleague
Richard La Plante
for his skills, encouragement, and for
taking time from his own book to edit mine.

Also by Terence Stamp:

Stamp Album

Double Feature

Foreword

I CANNOT CLAIM to know Terence Stamp well. We have collaborated on one film, attended one elaborate housewarming, and shared a total of two long meals. While we have been acquainted for a few years, the time we have spent one-on-one can be measured in hours.

I can make the case, however, that I know Terence Stamp intimately. The time one spends with him is not spent frivolously. That is not to say one doesn't laugh or dabble in trivia—I had to know, for example, if Samantha Eggar was everything I dreamed her to be—but the hours spent with Terence are rich, intense and rewarding. They are also efficient. Terence is a communicator—telling as much with a sigh as I could express in a paragraph. He never told me anything expressly about Ms. Eggar. Instead, he told me what she said about him in her autobiography. But the *way* he said it told me everything. Not what he knew, but what he felt. And in that moment I felt it too.

I suspect this was not an accident.

Terence has a deceptive face. And while this can be said about a great many actors, the deception often masks a disappointment—a revelation that an icon is merely human or, in certain cases, even less. Terence, however, has a face that hides his true nature. It is a lion's face—forged to communicate cool indifference. In truth, Terence is indifferent to being cool. At our first meeting, he arrived wearing shorts, a casual cotton shirt and pink rubber crocs. He was carrying several bags, having stopped to do some essential shopping on the way. My partners and I were prepared to meet Billy Budd, the Collector, the Limey, Zod—yet here we were, opposite someone who appeared to have almost forgotten the appointment. Within five minutes it became clear, however, that the aforementioned roles were mere facets of the man. He controlled the meeting from the outset—evading nothing while asking more questions than he answered. He was not auditioning for anything. We were.

I suspect this was not an accident.

Months later, we were on set in Berlin. Terence was dressed in the handmade suit of a retired German general circa 1944. The conversation turned to his younger obsession with fine clothes and the fascinating characters that cut for him. It was here that I met the Terence, and the London, of the 1960s— not through an anecdote, but a look of supreme confidence and control. It was also here that I met Tom Stamp's boy—laughing impishly, fleetingly, at a momentary lapse of discretion. That same day I met

Marlon Brando, not through some clichéd impression but a story of poignant self-deprecation.

Later, we were shooting a scene in which the protagonist's family fled to the basement during an air raid. The screenplay had been painstakingly researched and vetted by several experts—including eyewitnesses to many of the events. But only Terence observed that when he ran to his childhood basement during the Blitz, he did so with a sense of excitement and adventure. The finished scene is still the hardest one for me to watch. The tension we had intended is there sure enough, but how much better, how much truer might it have been with the protagonist watching in horror as his children play —oblivious to the bombs falling ever closer?

Einstein said "All learning is experience. Everything else is just information." And there is much to be learned from Terence Stamp—not just from the information he can impart, but from the experiences he is equipped uniquely to convey. Whether from the benefit of his years of experience or some innate inbred ability, Terence does not just relate experiences—he truly shares them. And he shares them truly.

It would be easy to say we live in an era when craft is losing ground to commerce. In fact, it would be hard to find the era when that wasn't easy to say. The truth is that craft has somehow always managed to survive *despite* commerce. It does so when hard-won knowledge and traditions are rediscovered and embraced by those seeking something deeper than commercial success alone. Perhaps you are here seeking such knowledge. Perhaps you are here to learn more about Billy Budd, the Collector, the Limey or Zod. Perhaps you are here strictly by chance. In any case, when you turn the page you will not enter this author's world as much as this author's world will enter you. From there, you will cease to be a reader. You will have become a witness, a curator, a vessel.

This is not an accident.

~ Christopher McQuarrie

Billy Budd, with Melvyn Douglas and Robert Ryan. 1962

THE ARTIST

The role of the artist, as I imagine it, has always been with us. Squatting around a fire, tired after a day of hunter/gathering, an individual is moved to stand up and re-enact something he has seen or heard. Or, maybe grabs a smouldering piece of wood and draws an outline of a bird in flight. The watchers are astounded. Ahh! It is the gasp of their collective vowel that affirms his spontaneous action. The first performing artist is born.

At this point in our communing, it would be lax of me if I didn't make clear how unlikely my embarkation on a life in showbiz was.

I was the eldest child of Tom Stamp, a stoker in the Merchant Navy (one up from a galley slave and known as a donkey-man) and a typewriter mechanic (at work erasing the "Made in Germany" part of the decal from the soon-to-be-for-sale Imperial machines). The signs did not bode well for a life of treading the boards.

I had made it to the local grammar school, in itself a small miracle. Yet, nevertheless, when my dad, God bless him, told me, "Son, people like us don't do things like that!" he wasn't kidding.

However. On one of my lengthy subterranean forays to work in London's West End, I made the decision to give it a go, spurred by the fact that if I failed, I would at least have tried. If I didn't make it as a performer, I might at least enjoy a life in show business.

Fifty years on, in the flash of an eye, I tell you this: No one can predict the workings of the universe—and while many may try, what I say is, power over circumstance or others is enslavement, yet power over oneself is mastery. The latter is what interests yours truly, and it's this we will be sharing in this tome.

* * *

"You can only rehearse for tomorrow, never the moment," is a truism that is often overlooked in the excitement of a young actor at the outset of his journey. As what is being discussed here are the benefits and how I encountered them in my life path, I hope to divide this into sections. What can be prepared and what can't. Wish me luck!

The initial problem is the craft itself. As Fred Astaire succinctly put it, "If you are aware of the work, you aren't working hard enough!" Whenever I see actors pulling faces or sticking their tongues out, I am bounced back into my seat at the theatre or cinema, the shared empathy severed. Nine times out of ten the surface mannerisms telegraphing a loss or lack of emotional surround.

When I studied to become an actor, drama schools only taught how to perform live, in the theatre, and I can only recall instruction as to the preparation, rarely the actual performance.

At the Webber Douglas Academy, we only got to tread the boards of their exquisite miniature theatre for dress and lighting rehearsals and a single performance. After which we moved on to the next term. I can't recall any discussion of when the curtain went up. So already I was being prepared for the Zen of the act. As they say in Japan, *ichi-go, ichi-e* —one moment, one chance!

There is a big divide between playing on the stage and on film. The difference, in my mind, is as between horses that race on the flat and those that jump. I'm sure the few that do both are as rare as their human counterparts.

I was fortunate that my own craft was rooted in the heat of theatre, unfurling in the presence of live audiences. And while it wasn't in my story to tread the boards for long, I have an undying admiration for those who do.

The adjective *great* is much bandied about these days by critics and public alike. I doubt any of them saw Laurence Olivier's Richard III live, or anything else of his, or of Laughton or Schofield. Any young actor embarking on a career in the classics should invest in a DVD of Olivier's Richard or Henry V and imagine what it must have been like to see him from the stalls.

Personally, I hit the wall when I progressed from weekly repertory (open Monday night, start re-hearsals for next week's play Tuesday morning) to fortnightly and monthly companies. Even the glamour and clamor of playing in London's West End found me struggling after the first week. All manner of the Method's emotional memory technique didn't cut it. I sought out older esteemed actors for their secrets to the night after night, eight shows a week lifestyle. Quizzed John Gielgud about his resilience in a long theatrical run.

"I don't feel secure until I know I'm in a play that's going to run for months," was all he offered. This from the man who'd played most of the Bard's leads —directed them, too.

I pressed, "But how do you *do* it?"

A look crossed his face that conveyed much but said little. Finally, he conceded.

"My dear Terence, it was different when I was starting out."

He gave me some tips on my vowel pronunciation.

Ralph Richardson was more helpful, albeit indirectly. I had been to see him and Gielgud in Harold Pinter's *No Man's Land* several times. On my third visit, the front of house manager offered me a copy of Pinter's text.

"I'm not here to fathom Pinter's dialogue," I replied. "I can't get enough of the two national treasures on the stage."

If I want to meet an actor, I usually go to a midweek matinee well into the run when most of the family and friends are long gone, and turn up backstage between shows, which I did with Sir Ralph. Acknowledging my persistence, he extended an invitation to have a drink with him at his house a few days later. I took him up on it and duly made my way to his residence overlooking Regent's Park. He escorted me to his study, proudly displaying en route the elevator he'd recently installed.

What immediately grabbed my attention was a series of large handwritten paper foolscaps fixed to the picture rails bearing samples of Pinter's conundrums. Seeing my obvious curiosity, he said with a wave, "These are the lines I am working on this week!"

I didn't need to ask my question; three months into the run and he's still mining for new meaning. When I had been sitting comfortably in the stalls at the Wyndhams Theatre watching the knights of the English stage perform, I had experienced a shift in my awareness. As though what I had been observing some distance away was transmuted into an action inside myself, actually inside the field of my aware-ness. It was accompanied by a feeling akin to joy. Later, going over the event in my mind, I thought it must have been the result of a presence on stage completely immersed in what he was doing yet simultaneously open enough to accommodate the collective energy of the audience.

The great Ralph Richardson, one of the few with absolute mastery over stage and screen, didn't tap into the abstract by accident.

Could it be that any artist worthy of the title turns the spectator back on him or herself? Or, put another way, allows us to feel that what we are looking at is also what is looking.

As Dionysus in Greek amphitheatre

THE BREATH

On a relative scale of importance, we can exist without food for about ninety days, without water for seven, but air is the condition under which we are here. If we overlook for the moment the different ways we shrug off this mortal coil, we are left with the fact that when breath leaves the body, its run is over. It wouldn't be an exaggeration that without breath we are a mass of skin and bones.

In my own case, I didn't give breath a thought until I landed on my feet at the Webber Douglas Academy of Speech and Drama and realised I couldn't get through Shakespeare's stanzas by breathing in the slapdash manner that had got me thus far.

Initially, I marked the text where I should take a breath without losing the sense of the delivery. Then someone told me that Frank Sinatra, as a young man, swam regularly to improve the dimension of his breathing. Don't know the truth of this, but I was very into Frank at the time—*Songs For Swingin' Lovers*, in particular. I started paying extra interest to his phrasing, and my interest was aroused in expanding the scope and compass of my own breath.

The scholarship I had won, making it possible to study at Webber full time, not only paid my fees but gave me eight pounds a month to live on. This barely covered my rent. Most of the time I lived on my wits, and weighed in at 10 stone 4 pounds; hence the gossip among the girl students, not completely untrue, that Terence was anybody's for a boiled egg and bowl of soup!

Nevertheless, I began swimming on Saturdays at the Marshall Street public baths and jogging to school when I didn't have the fare for the Underground. From these pedestrian beginnings, my interest in breath and breathing grew and has continued to this day, training the diaphragm, sustaining the note and projecting the voice.

* * *

In the beginning was the Word. Certain ancient metaphysical orders that specialise in such things complete the saying by adding, *and the Word was Hu.* Hence the word *Hu-man* or *human.* The original meaning of the word *man* was *mind,* and *Hu, divine.* The *Hu* in question is the original sound, heard in the water rippling over stones, the soughing of the wind, even the tolling of a bell. As the first vibrations from silence became sound—before colour and shape—particular significance is paid to the voice.

Today, performing artists rely increasingly on microphones to fill an auditorium, and less emphasis is paid to the natural voice production.

Some years ago, Edward Fox and I were hired to take part in a production of the ancient Greek play *The Bacchae*. He was cast as Pentheus, me as Dionysus. It was to be part of a series on the history of the theatre, filmed for television. Edward and I got to shoot in Greece and played on the stage of the most complete auditorium in Dodona.

At the time this play was first performed in the open theatre where we were doing it, the actors wore masks. Mr. Fox and myself did not—although the makeup department created for me a blond Bo Derek style wig, which topped a pale blue makeup (as often used to depict deity in Indian sacred paintings), to which was added a heavy circle of maroon eye shadow, giving the effect of ancient theatrical ancestors, whose eyes must have glinted out from their masks.

Standing astride the earthen stage ready and waiting for the perfect pre-sunset light, I was struck by the remoteness of the 2000-year-old theatre. Pitched where it was for the perfect acoustics and sight lines, the only sound on stage was the breeze and the clanking of goat bells as the creatures wended their way home.

In the days when *The Bacchae* was being performed to its ancient blond audience, the main transport for man was by foot. Keen spectators would have to have stomped miles across the countryside, even bringing their goats with them. What were the writers and performers offering these pilgrims?

For the moment, we can take the text as a given. Which would have been appreciated without masks if spoken by the trained Brad Pitt of the day in these exquisite surrounds. Yet the masks are a fact. So, taking away the facial characteristics of the players, we are left with the voice and the presence of the performer. It was that way then and, regardless of technological advances, still is, the essence of the art.

Discovered with Discoverer. Press conference, 1962

THE FIRST TAKE

During my times with Marlon Brando, at his peak the finest actor of the modern era, we often revisited this very topic.

I had waited my whole show biz career to work with Marlon, and in '77, the chance arrived. It was only a moment in front of the camera, not that, really. He'd been hired reputedly for a million bucks for twelve days' work, and on the thirteenth (which he gave them 'gratis') we faced each other on Krypton. Sadly, I was only his eye line, not even in the shot. Probably, Marlon wasn't expecting a lot of input from me doing my lines off camera, and his demeanour and approach was casual. On "action," I gave it my all; eight years without a job, fresh from the ashram in the East where awareness was the benchmark, I unholstered the Magnum I'd been packing since my arrival on set. Even before my outburst singed his eyebrows, he acknowledged my commitment: No ashes from yesterday in this take, only Jor-El and Zod on the high wire. I experienced the energy of his *Waterfront* Terry, the magnetism of Emiliano Zapata. But it was offstage he gave me pause.

It is hard to get Brando to be serious; he was just the funniest guy I've ever met. On our first day on the set, probably to offset the silliness of our outfits, he strolled over to me and, pointing to the two Eurasian girls he appeared to be travelling with he said, "See those girls?"

I looked across. They giggled together. I nodded.

"They want your dick."

"What about your dick, Marlon?"

"They've had my dick. Now they're interested in yours."

That more than broke the ice.

We stayed close for the remainder of his stay at Pinewood, giggling, laughing, gossiping; he was naturally comical and a storyteller. Didn't tell jokes, the humour came out of the way he saw life, and he was rarely serious. Yet the exchange I recall puts in perspective a lot of the wild stories that circulate about him.

We discussed our approach to performing, and basically he acknowledged the domain of the medium belonged to the director, for whom he had devised a test. On the first day, Marlon would produce a take in which he invested himself. If the director didn't feel it or see it and requested more takes, Marlon stopped trying. He just coasted through the film, going through the motions and picking up the cheque.

I know the feeling. I don't have the clout or the stature to pull a Brando, but I sure know the feeling.

When you are working with a Wyler, a Fellini, an Ustinov, or a Soderbergh, they love actors who nail it on the first take. It was a buzz to hear Soderbergh say after take one, "We're in the wrong place, folks."

Those directors trust their intuition and their intuition trusts them. They love what they do and don't waste time, energy, or money. It's all in the camera. You can imagine how it makes you feel to have a William Wyler or a Federico Fellini squeezed under the camera at one with you between "action" and "cut." You can live without imagining the opposite; a director in another room glued to his video playback on morning number one of a shoot, hollering through his megaphone, "We'll go again" after something electric has passed through you. It happens a lot these days. Directors who are so in-secure they shoot everything from everywhere, leaving nothing to chance in the editing room. An editor pal of mine told me recently he was presented with two hours of rushes to cut into a five-minute sequence.

Matt Damon and I were working together last year and he told me something reassuring. He was being directed by Clint Eastwood. At one point, he asked Clint if he could do a second take. Clint said something to the effect of, "D'you want to keep the whole crew waiting? I'm happy with your first take; let's move on." Of course, Matt jumped at the chance to work with him again. But, then, Mr. Eastwood earned his spurs in front of the camera and knows how to get the best from his actors. That's why he cast them.

* * *

In Khalil Gibran's book *The Prophet*, he writes about a leaf on a green tree, which turns red, thereby changing the whole tree. I read this book when I was seventeen; and the idea of an individual being an integral part of the whole and capable of changing the totality by bringing about a change in his self really resonated with me.

It appears the artist effects change by his work, yet he is not primarily concerned with trying because at some level he has experienced the ease and immediacy of the creative act. All artists—be they poets, writers, composers, lyricists, musicians, or painters—have felt this. When it all becomes very easy, ideas flow unimpaired. The hand moves as if by itself—the struggling and blocks of the past, a dream, the voice of unity through the diverse. More than one creative artist has commented, "I was not in the way of the work."

This is what Brando meant when he said he invested himself in a take; himself being the clear awareness from which his feelings arose. The presence of the very best of oneself, which cannot be summoned, yet can be awaited. Once it has announced itself, it is a thrill like no other. Hence the aforementioned adage: You can rehearse for tomorrow; not the moment.

This is probably what Fellini was referring to when he told me he viewed himself as a midwife. As the film could enter this dimension via anyone, he always left a little corner open for this happenstance.

As an actor, this feeling of absolute awareness is sufficient to itself; it is only when the realisation comes that the magic moment has been missed by the director and not printed, that there is a sense of utter loss.

Jor-El and Zod, 1978

ARCHETYPES

Actors usually fall into one of four archetypes. It goes without saying that every individual has everything at his fingertips. But one type relates predominately to the physical; another to the mind; a third, the emotions, and there are those who consciously blend them all.

If you've spent your formative years lifting weights, you are going to draw physical roles to you. I once heard an interview with a young actor who explained that he made a list of thoughts he was going to run through his brain when in character. An actress I once worked with was so consumed by her emotions she had no sense of where her mark was. It takes all sorts, as my Granny Kate used to say. Your career as an artist is the gymnasium where all facets of yourself are developed and blended.

One of the reasons Hamlet is considered the hoop through which every male actor should jump is that it demands all dimensions of the actor. It was not a role I had the confidence to take on when I was young. The legendary American actor John Barrymore came to London when he was 25 and gave his

Prince of Denmark at the Haymarket Theatre. I am told both Laurence Olivier and John Gielgud came to wonder, but on returning to New York, Barrymore's performance went unsung, as he was considered *just* a movie star.

I have always tried to mimic the work ethic of those I look up to. The opera singer Joan Sutherland, La Stupenda, as she became known, as she came from humble origins in Australia, yet worked on her voice every day for the sixty years she bestrode the world of every kind of opera. Yes, she had unique vocal chords and an amazing head, whose whole facemask reverberated with sound. But she soldiered on, practising daily through anonymity, fame, penury and wealth. If you were born with a splendid voice, appreciate it. If your voice is light, thin, develop that which is not yet apparent.

My own early efforts, swimming lengths underwater, was my way of letting the body know what I wanted of it. I do the same today. I consider every moment spent in conscious development capital in the bank. Of course, you can spend your days trying to put others in spaces that suit you, trying to rig your circumstances to make yourself comfortable. My admiration is for those who turn themselves into an electromagnet and see what it attracts.

In New York last year, I was working with George Nolfi, who was directing his own screenplay from Philip K. Dick's short story "The Adjustment Bureau." He drew attention to something that had never occurred to me—that a lot of actors allow their success to make them soft. The first class flights, chauffeured cars, lull them into not wanting to dig deep. They go off the boil.

It didn't occur to me because as my success was so unlikely, it's still a treat that show business embraced me at all. I approach my work as though every job is my first but, more likely, my last.

It probably stems from an insecurity I inherited from my dad. He was unusually good looking, with a wicked sense of humour, not unlike Marlon, and I don't think he ever had trouble with anyone. But in spite of physical strength, looks, and humour, he was inwardly insecure. A fact I only realised later in life.

On the evening of the opening night of my debut film, Peter Ustinov's screen version of Herman Melville's seafaring saga *Billy Budd*, I had arranged for my parents to go to the premiere. They were still living in deepest Plaistow (Plaistow's main claim to fame was West Ham United Football team) and an hour before the affair, Dad announced he didn't want to go. He was something of a stoic and never explained the whys of anything. It was only when it became evident that wild horses wouldn't keep Mum from attending, and she readied herself to go alone, that he changed into a clean shirt and agreed to accompany her.

It turned out to be a night like no other. My date, Samantha Eggar, and I were snapped by paparazzi in the foyer of the Leicester Square Theatre with Tom and Ethel on arrival. The film had already been reviewed as a master work by Ustinov and the screening went extremely well. As the Stamp posse came down the stairs from the circle into the lobby, we discovered that few of the audience had left. The foyer was so packed, most had to lift their hands over their heads to applaud our descent.

I can't imagine what must have been going through my parents' heads at that moment as there was certainly no time for chat, as Peter and his wife, Suzanne Cloutier, took us up to the White Elephant in Curzon Street for a late supper.

The occasion was so warm, vibrant, and unexpected that my own recall is a little hazy, but I do remember that my dad always appreciated great comics, and in Peter Ustinov he came upon one of the best. Not on stage or TV, but sitting across from him. When Peter discovered Tom wasn't averse to the sherbet, he made sure Dad's glass was always topped up. And when Dad discovered his own one-liners were cracking Peter up, it was apparent the universal law of like kinds had brought the two together.

The festivities went well into the night and it was 3:00 A.M. before Sam and I dropped Tom and Ethel off back in Plaistow and we sped back to her pad in Sydney Street.

Curiously, it was some years later that Mum told me her end of the adventure. When the limo had dropped them off at the two-up two-down in Chadwin Road, she had asked Tom what they should do.

"You make us a pot of tea. We'll have a cuppa, then you can get your head down, and I'll get off to work!"

Which is what they did. I should mention that Dad went to work on a push bike, and the Isle of Dogs, where his tug was moored, was a good five or six miles from their house. So although he missed a night's sleep when he caught the early tide, he probably wasn't feeling any pain by permission of the 1906 cognac Ustinov had treated him to. Time and tide wait for no man—even if it's at 5:30 A.M.

I never asked Mum what they chatted about over the pot of tea, which was remiss of me as Mum would no doubt have remembered it word for word.

Flash forward to the mid-Eighties. I had found work hard to get for most of the Seventies, but I am back in London, a lot older and a little wiser.

On the afternoon in question, I am returning from the street market in Soho to the north gate of the block I am still residing in, when a tall, powerfully built guy about my own age stops me.

"You Tom Stamp's boy?" he asks.

It is not an opening I've heard before.

"I am."

We stop on the Mappin and Webb corner of Regent Street.

"Did you know my dad?"

"I was his lad. On the Bronco. Made his tea."

He has the remnants of a Cockney accent, the lilt of London fog in his delivery.

"When was that?"

"Early Sixties. I was an apprentice lighterman."

"Good number," I say. It was an esteemed profession, something my dad never aspired to, involving a lengthy apprenticeship as it did.

"What's your name then?"

"Robert Lockwood. Bob, to you."

"You weren't on the tug the day after my first film opened, were you, Bob?"

Both my parents had died. It was suddenly important, this casual meeting with one of my dad's workmates.

"Certainly was," he replied. "'Course, your dad never mentioned it, but when we docked, must have been after five o'clock, one of the geezers from another tug was clutching the early edition of the *Evening Standard*, and on the front page is a picture of you with your mum and dad. 'What's all this, Tom,' the geezer asks. Tom studied the paper. 'Ee's a very lucky boy,' was all he said." Apparently, the subject was never broached again.

At the time the incident was relayed to me, I felt disappointed, hungry as I was for details. I had lived my whole life without knowing how my dad felt about my success.

Yet, as I write, I understand his succinct response. I *was* lucky. I still feel lucky. I am already older than my dad. I live my life as if every moment is my last, but at the same time, with the feeling I will live forever.

Disciple and Master, 20 years on.

MORE ABOUT THE BREATH
(INDIA)

In a long career, there are invariably lulls. You either start late—Jack Nicholson didn't get discovered until well into his thirties; neither did Michael Caine—or, there is a parched stretch in the middle, as in Cary Grant's case, and my own. It's tough, as at the time there is no certainty the final curtain hasn't fallen.

I coped by travelling, and drew inspiration from Muhammad Ali. On my first trip to New York, I was up front on a big TWA jet. There was a lot of commotion at the rear and I strolled back to catch the action. It was the then Cassius Clay and his extensive entourage. I had seen him in action a few nights earlier at the Arsenal Stadium, when he'd taken Henry Cooper down. He looked alight, sitting there, talking with his hands the way many fighters do, laughing and animated, lit from within. His charisma was overwhelming. After that, I kept up with his career. Hearing somewhere that during his time away from the ring—when he was banned for not fighting in Vietnam—he stayed very fit so that whenever the call came he would be ready at an hour's notice, if need be.

When, during my long sojourn in the East, the weeks became months, the months became years and my hair became noticeably grey, I would recall Ali's discipline. Whether it was the breathing practices that strengthened my core and stretched my lungs or the long Tai Chi forms that complemented my coordination and kept my tendons supple, my mantra became, "This will refine my performances when the call comes."

I knew my mother was worried by my lack of work. I kept afloat by letting go of the antiques, paintings, carpets, and wine I had accrued during the moneyed years. And when I returned to England to mastermind these sales, I would take Mum to the Soda Fountain at Fortnum and Mason's, before it was "restored." The waitresses were all working class ladies; and even when their permutation football pool came up trumps and they shared half a million quid, none of them gave up their job. They liked Mum, who had been a barmaid in between kids, and she liked them. I always tried to look my best and give her the impression that I was still the rock on whom the family could rely. It wasn't until after she passed away that I realised it was quite the opposite. She was, in fact, the rock upon whom I relied.

On one of my visits to India, I had an inkling of how harsh the future decades would be. I certainly failed to see the symbolism of my neighbours, the Beatles, giving their last concert on the roof of their Savile Row headquarters. I paid my respects to them before boarding my taxi to Heathrow, on what I felt might be a life changing experience. Of course, my life's story had already been reset. Like most of us, I was largely unaware of the implications a single degree of change would bring to my life's compass. I was to be as surprised as a ship's captain who sets sail for the Hebrides, makes a tiny error on day one, and winds up in the Faroe Isles.

If I'd known then what I know now, it wouldn't have been necessary to hurl myself around the globe. As Judy Garland's character says in the *Wizard of Oz*, you only discover after your journey what was always there in your own backyard.

India in 1969 was as chaotic as it is now. Yet the nature of its inhabitants and their tolerance of their fellow man made a big impression on me. Foreigners such as myself were thin on the ground, as the exodus East had only just begun. I had an array of encounters with complete strangers who seemed to know why I was there before I did. As a result, I was enriched by the wisdom of both the main faiths, Hinduism and Islam. I guess I was unusually open to the moment, as every moment presented to me a mind-blowingly new impression, which didn't have space for memory or projections.

One evening, I returned to my hotel room in Agra after seeing the Taj Mahal by a full moon, and the night man was turning down my bed. He must have spotted my amber beads, as he returned later with a small copy of the *Bhagavad Gita*. This small act led to me being invited to a ceremony at his dwelling, where his daughter, who was having her ninth birthday, was being initiated into the practice of "complete breath," something the Brahmin caste did when their offspring reached the age of nine. I was impressed; this wasn't a social order of singers and stroller players, but artists of another order: scholars, philosophers who studied ancient texts of learning and practised them for thousands of years; artists of another order, indeed.

It's tricky when you start altering the patterns of something that you have done unconsciously since birth, but learning to breathe fully, enlivening every atom in the body, can only enrich your life. The only word of caution I was given was not to hold breath in my head, whatever the practice.

I don't really subscribe to just reading about breathing practices, but once your eyes are open to this mysterious flow, the source of which no one knows, you are bound to encounter someone who knows more than you and his or her advice will be your next step. There is a saying in the East that if you are a vegetarian and you travel to a new place, you will inevitably meet another vegetarian. The same law applies if you are a thief.

During the afternoon I spent with the Brahmin family in Agra, I was taught a yogic breathing practice called Kapala Bati, which translates as "shining skull." In the late sixties, Kapala Bati was an appropriate spur for an flagging actor down on his luck.

Since then, and through the years, I have continued the practice. Finding that it removes stale air from the body, exercises the diaphragm, and increases the lung capacity required for long lines of dialogue and cold swims underwater.

If we return for a moment to "In the beginning was the Word," it wouldn't be a stretch to say "In the beginning was the breath." So, while sound for us is the audible manifestation of breath, it is also how we manage to stay here.

'Bad Boy Troy', *Far From the Madding Crowd*, 1967

OUT OF TIME

In the world of sensitives, those folks who are open to extrasensory perception, the individuals who hear the sound of the spheres, or music of the spheres, are considered of a different octave than those who see into the world unseen, as their degree of sensitivity is closer to the breath.

I can't lay much claim to any of these attributes, yet the occasions when my sensitivity showed itself are indelible.

When I was little, I was always allowed to play in the street. We didn't have a garden, as such, and the streets were different then, anyway. Even during the war, if an air-raid siren went off, I was told to run into the nearest house. Toward the end of the war, we moved farther east to our house in Plaistow, which, these days, is considered one of the most dangerous areas in London.

In 1942, Chadwin Road, E13 was a peaceful suburb. Nobody on our street owned a car, and the road was our main playground. Halfway up the street was a shop called Price's, a family-owned grocery. The thing that separated the Price household was that they had a refrigerator, in which they made ice cubes flavoured with something, which they sold for a penny each in summer. Everyone used coal, and the horse-drawn wagon from which the coalman delivered his sacks fired up all the hearths in our neighbourhood. Of course, we regularly had serious fogs.

One afternoon after school, I was given a shilling and told to buy a loaf from Price's. I opened the front door to discover a fog had formed. It was a real pea-souper. As it was a regular occurrence, I didn't give it too much thought, although when I put my hand in front of my face, I couldn't see it. Even these kinds of fogs didn't grind the East End to a halt. The conductors on the trolley buses had flares, which they lit, and walked down the road in front of their drivers.

I set off on my errand, walking with one foot in the gutter and the other on the kerb to give me my bearings, but after bumping into a lamp-post (gas, but unlit), I measured three long strides into what I judged to be the middle of the road and continued on my errand. After a few minutes, I completely lost my bearings—and two things happened. Through the fog I felt snowflakes in my face and on my head. I recall sticking out my tongue to catch some flakes on it, and then: blank.

It was as if I had disappeared. I guess thought simply stopped. There was only the cold on my face and the beating of my heart. I have no idea how much time passed during the curious absence, and I assume the body stopped walking, for when I returned, so to speak, I became aware of the light from Price's window in the distance, which I began walking toward.

Nothing untoward accompanied these moments out of time. On the contrary, whenever they came to mind, I had a nice feeling. It wasn't something I spoke of; a secret. And like a wish, diluted when shared.

Another unfamiliar occurrence happened when I was about five years old. For many generations, London's working class were invited to the fields of Kent for the annual hop harvest. The wives and kids were billeted in corrugated huts close to the hop fields, while the men-folk continued their jobs in London, sometimes travelling down at weekends.

I guess it was a tough working holiday for the womenfolk, but for us it was heaven, our only inter-action with the country. Our farm was aptly named New Barns. There was a country bus, green, which stopped at the Woolpack Pub a hundred yards or so from the common where we lived, but it was notoriously irregular, and the mile and half walk to the village, Yalding, became a familiar trek. As the hop-picking was a six-day a week affair, we kids were entrusted to pick up staples from Yalding. Our mum or one of the aunts would do the weekly shopping with our help.

Yalding itself comprised a main road and a T-junction with a medieval bridge over the Medway River, a bakery, a post office, a pub, and a general store. The general store was fascinating to me, primarily because of how trusting the owners were. Newly baked bread, hocks of ham, huge wedges of cheese, jars of pickles were all on open and unpro-tected display. I understand that a few seasons after the blitz, when the marauding "hoppers" from London markedly depleted their on-the-counter displays, stock was relocated to less tempting acces-sibility. On the morning in question, however, it was still on display and uncovered. Our Aunt Maude was in charge of us. Maude was the youngest of the Perrott sisters and I always saw her as the prettiest. She also let us get away with more stuff, and on the walk into town turned a blind eye to the foraging of wild blackberries, damsons, and even apples whose branches hung over the walled gardens. So when the little motley crew arrived, our hands were stained purple, on top of the hop resin that seemed to accumulate on the fingertips of all who regularly picked them.

I don't actually remember feeling hungry when we entered... which wasn't usually the case, but I mention it in view of what happened next. As I came through the front door, I inhaled the shop's aroma, a collage of all the gastronomic perfumes I associated with good food, but stronger, more intense than on previous visits, even when I had been ravenous. Which was most of the time, due to country air and its increased oxygen, growing noticeably, and the daily proximity to the harvested hops and the residue they left on our fingers that seemed to permeate everything we touched, including all foodstuffs that went into our mouths. What we didn't know then was that the hop, Humulus lupulus, is a close relation to cannabis sativa, the grass that is much inhaled today. The aroma that day was overpowering and stopped me in my Wellington boots. I have a tendency to increase sensation, which is so ingrained I am no longer aware of it, but on this particular occasion, I didn't even close my eyes to center myself on my sense of smell. I just stood in the doorway, inhaling every breath as though it was my last. The aroma underwent a change; the aroma of cheese and spam segued into something resembling new-mown hay, and before the shop returned to normal, the periphery became an attar of rose without any source I could see. I seemed to exist in a timeless void, awash in this sweet scent, barely aware of Maude's soft dry hand taking hold of mine as she entered the shop. I realised later that this entire event could have only taken a mini-second, another step out of time.

Julie and Terry with Phil Donahue, during a break
in shooting *Far From the Madding Crowd*

THE VOICE

In 1961, I found myself in a state of flux. I had played the title role in *Billy Budd*, yet due to wrinkles in the distribution, the film hadn't actually been seen. I was in limbo.

A young producer I had met named Kaplan had lent me his Jaguar convertible, the XK120. I hadn't yet passed my test. In truth, I had failed it twice. A chum I had at the time, a young actor named Clive Colin Bowler, quipped that I could drive fine, but I should confine myself to getaway cars.

Of course, it didn't stop us tooling around the West End in the XK with the top down. On one such jaunt, we were pulled over near Trafalgar Square by a cop on a motorbike. He got off his Triumph—they still rode English bikes in the Sixties—and strolled toward us. He was a big man. I clambered out of the Jag. In those days, it was a regulation that you would only be considered for the Force if you were over five feet, eight inches. The guy approaching me looked more like six foot eight.

The expression written on the Goliath's face, squeezed under his helmet was saying, "I got you, you skinny flash fuck!"

I knew I was banged to rights, with no license, no insurance and no escape.

Yet as I engaged in "Good afternoon, Officer," or a similarly mundane opening, a very extraordinary thing happened. The voice that materialised was not my own. Or, rather it was *so* my own that a thrill went through my whole being. Not a voice I had ever heard before... yet closer to me than my jugular vein. And of a quality that is hard to put into words, for it was somehow connected to everything and everybody. At the sound of this voice, which driven by nerves and adrenaline resonated deep from my gut, the giant's expression softened. He didn't speak. I did, but what I said was superfluous. It was the mellifluous tone that was mesmerising him. I extended my hand. He took off his gauntlet glove and we shook. Then I stepped back into the car and drove off. Clive Colin didn't comment on the silvery delivery and never did. Neither did I. Yet the happening gave me pause. Substantial pause, for I knew I had been party to something immensely larger than, yet not separate from, me.

As the years passed, many of which I spent "resting," I used the time to study. I happened on the term

Original Face and likened my speed cop event to Original Voice. That's how I felt about it, anyway.

It is the nature of my mind that once it has conceptualized something it comes up with a steady stream of ideas: If I could harness this delivery, utilise it at will, I could become a unique performer, Mesmer-like. But it wasn't like that, and deep down I knew it. Slowly, whilst I never forgot it, I lost touch with Clive Colin Bowler and couldn't confirm if he'd even heard the exchange. The memory faded as a pressed violet in an unread book.

It might have ended there had not another incident involving another car and another owner taken place that allowed me to see, or at least hope, that maybe I was the vehicle used for this magic that had meshed with my psyche and drew me in.

Seventeen years pass. I am in a relationship with a girl I'll call Ms. Edge. I am starting *Superman* I and II with Richard Donner. Who, I must say, is a prince— with such an infectious roar of a laugh that he is getting the best out of all of us in the face of gumption-sapping difficulties.

On a free Saturday afternoon, Ms. Edge is driving us around town on a weekend shop. Ms. Edge is one of a few lady drivers who see themselves at the wheel of a Formula One motorcar, but at present she is content with the anthracite Beetle convertible, with the top down and heater on. We have safely bypassed Harrods and are cruising along opposite Brompton Square when she says, "Oh, Stamp. I could pick up my dress at the cleaners but I don't have the ticket. Could you ask for it for me?" I glance at her intense profile. She always watches the road. Acknowledging my lack of response—this is a regular occurrence—she says in her helpless girly voice, "I've lost the ticket."

The car stops outside the dry cleaners. As it is a main thoroughfare, I expect her to stay in the car, but she switches off the engine and follows me in.

As I start my mundane, yet practiced request, I hear coming from my lips the Original Voice, with the accompanying tremor throughout the body.

"...The name is Edge; it's a white woollen number..."

The line is hardly in the air when the girl returns with Carol's dress on a padded hanger in a cellophane shroud. I produce some cash, carefully, mindful that any movement could break the spell.

The Voice expresses its silken thanks as we leave the shop. By the time we are in the car it has faded. Gone. Yet, again, it isn't commented on as she places her dress on the backseat and we drive off.

It had been the same and different. No danger. No expedient circumstances yet equally thrilling and mysterious. I wanted it back. I wanted to be able to call upon the Voice at any time, to have it under my complete control.

Throughout the years, the finest voice coaches get to know me well. A few offer minor adjustments. One instructs me how to strengthen the tip of my tongue after discovering I could pronounce *contract*, yet couldn't enunciate the plural, *contracts*, without skipping the second "c."

Usually after a few sessions, they enquire as to exactly what I am looking for. A question I didn't feel at liberty to answer. If I cannot find it naturally in their teachings, why define it?

I finally hear of an esteemed singing maestro who teaches Bel canto and has turned Lyric baritones into tenors. He is hard to get to see, but once in, doesn't throw me out. Still, nothing inspires the return of the revered voice although the maestro's lessons keep me focused while I wait.

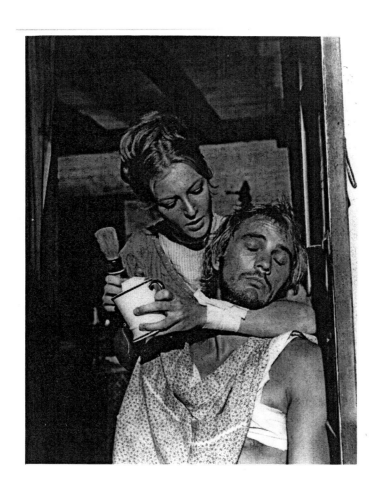
Being shaved by Joanna Pettet in *Blue*, 1968.

Moab, Utah. *Blue*, 1968

THE WORDS

The words, or as one of Britain's finest old thespians told me when I asked for his wisdom on the subject, *"The wordies. Learn the wordies."*

At the time, I had a sneaking suspicion he could be pulling my leg. Yet why would he? I was an avid young actor, starting out, in my second term at drama school. No. He was an admired actor, revered by many. It was a stroke of luck to catch him on the Metropolitan Line of London's Underground.

When I had initially engaged him, he had paused. It was a long pause, interminable, it had seemed to me at the time. Then came the response, in his strange, unique delivery. Once heard, never forgotten. "The wordies, learn the wordies." The pause had been significant, the opposite of my mental insecurities. His advice had contained unspoken wisdom. But at the same time, it was wisdom I could grasp and practice, allowing the best in me to come forth. Wilfrid Lawson was his name, and he was a prince among actors.

Learning the words was always tough for me. Most actors have difficulties, but mine seemed doubly tough. It meant revisiting my formal schooling. Overcoming the mental barriers I had erected to prevent the sensation of being hemmed in, squash-ed. The learning-by-rote system of education has a lot to answer for in my book.

I hadn't boosted my spontaneity by alcohol or drugs so I knew my central nervous system was in pretty good shape. My emotional canvas was what I needed to address. I needed to have easier access to my feelings when I was under the cosh between action and cut.

Then one of those intuitive leaps happened. I had come across a magazine someone had left on one of London's beautiful Routemasters. (One of Britain's greatest functional designs, scrapped by some heathen of a mayor who claimed anyone who got rid of them would have to be an idiot—which he did when elected. Sound familiar?) It concerned a young man whose right hemisphere in his brain had been irreparably damaged. As the two hemispheres have different functions, the result was conclusively marked. With sight, for example, the right hemi-sphere only sees the whole picture, the left, only particulars. The damaged young man, after his accident, could only see someone's nose or mouth or eye. Not the whole face.

I had been born very left-handed. I hadn't been compelled to use my right hand at all, but found myself in a very right handed world. Scissors, learning to tie my shoelaces, had presented me with all kinds of difficulties. Learning to read had been an ongoing nightmare. Aged 14 and already fashion conscious, tying a double Windsor knot in my school tie had taken an age to master.

My continuing failure to learn from the detail up had serious ramifications on my progress in academia. When I sat the dreaded Scholarship or Eleven Plus, I felt as if I had only just learned to read. I considered my entry in the local grammar school was by Divine Intervention.

Even early forays in drama had been laced with trauma. Aged 15, when I should have been preparing for the GCE, I was cast in the role of a 55-year-old in a play by Somerset Maughan: *The Sacred Flame.* Whilst it was an amateur production, my failure to master the seemingly endless dialogue had ensured a terrifying opening night at the local Town Hall, packed, needless to say.

My intuitive leap informed me that if I mindfully started to use my right hand and feature it in my daily life, this would entail my left hemisphere being brought more into play.

Slowly, slowly catchy monkey, I made an easy, non-threatening start. Combing my hair, brushing my teeth with both hands. When I became proficient, I moved onto something new.

By the time I made the western *Blue* (my future ex-wife's favoured film of mine) I was faster at drawing my six-shooter with my right hand.

During my second term at the Webber Douglas Academy, however, I was cast as Iago in Shake-speare's *Othello*. I somehow felt this was no ordinary event, and figured if I were to pull it off I would have to know the lines almost before rehearsals were underway. I compelled myself to memorise a page of Iago every day. Whenever I had one page down, I would begin my day by facing myself in a corner and reciting out loud whatever I had learned. If I dried somewhere I would go back over the lines to ensure I had them before embarking on the new page. It was a slog. I copied out difficult soliloquies five or six times, marking out where I would need a breath.

The system at Webber was different from other drama schools. We were in four different productions per term with only a single production of each.

When the curtain went up, I began what I later realised was the first spontaneous performance of my new career. My lines and cues had almost become second nature. Alongside the functioning of the breath, diaphragm, vocal chords, and everything else involved in everyday speech (which is perfect example of spontaneity) I had been able to add learned lines and regimented breathing, and still leave enough space for impromptu emotions and their intonations previously hidden in text, by the Bard himself, and enlivened by the breath in the dynamic of performance. I can liken it to learning to drive. No automatic cars in my youth. How difficult it had been to even change gears: foot off the accelerator, down with the clutch, glance in the rear view mirror, control the steering, manipulate the gear stick, the accelerator pedal depressed as the clutch pedal is released. Yet, after a few days, all taken care of by the intelligence of the body, allowing me to speed around the Formula One circuit when the curtain goes up or the clapper board snaps down.

It doesn't get easier. If my outings are anything to go by, it gets more demanding. Don't be taken in by the flesh coloured earphones that allow an off-stage assistant to read the lines directly into the ear piece. Your returns are usually related to your investment.

I should mention at this point that most of my friends consider me barking. Barking mad, that is. As I have usually done things the opposite way to everybody else; but the fact is that the path that I have been taken along is as unique as yours. You don't have to go to India, become a vegetarian, study

Tai Chi or whirl like a dervish. All you have to do is wake up in the morning and appreciate that this moment is yours. Yours alone. It won't be repeated. You will never pass this way again. Give it your best shot. Everything you need is in this moment.

With Celia Hammond at the *Blue* premiere, 1968.

THE MUSE

Everyone exists in the present. Everyone has presence. The role of the artist is to merge the two. For this, equanimity is needed. If this had been made clear to me at the outset, I wouldn't have needed the disciplines I subjected myself to.

Have you ever noticed how tough it is to listen to most politicians making speeches? The few who can grab you are the exceptions that prove the rule.

I had the pleasure of meeting President Clinton recently and asked him how he did it. I met him at a gathering in London's Guildhall, and he invited my girlfriend and me to his suite at the Ritz. We were lucky to find a black cab quickly and arrived first, so we had him to ourselves until his colleagues showed up. He has that innate intelligence that allows others the space to reveal where they're at before he says much. I have always appreciated the artist in him. So I addressed him as such and asked him how he dealt with the changing dynamic of every new audience. He didn't answer immediately, so I added that I never wrote speeches, preferring to get on stage, sense the qualities of the audience, and trust the inspiration would be there for me.

He explained that as he mostly wrote his speeches himself, including the one we had previously listened to, he was completely familiar with the material, but always arrived early to get the feel, the ambience of the audience so that he could improvise, albeit tethered to his material if he wasn't inspired.

I found his explanation reassuring in the way it is when something agrees with your own view. Yet he convinced me he encompassed the energy of the audience by engaging them in the moment.

Cary Grant often changed his dialogue on the first take, to "freshen them up a bit."

Marlon Brando was an opposite to my method of learning the lines well enough to forget them. On one of the days when we were both on set, I saw him fiddling around with a bit of paper, which he kept pulling out of his pocket, looking, mouthing a few words and returning it. He looked like a young actor just starting out rather than a giant of the screen.

"What are you up to, Brando?" I asked.

He pointed to a sizeable card hanging from the ceiling behind the camera; lit with its own light on which his dialogue was writ large.

"I can't remember my lines anymore, so I have to read them. I thought if I could memorise my opening line," he pulled his piece of paper from his pocket to show me, "I could say it on a turn toward the camera, make it look more natural."

"How you gonna' do Macbeth or Lear, if you can't learn Superman's dad?"

"I've learnt them already," he retorted without a pause.

As I said before, he wasn't a man to whom serious talk came easy. Yet he often quoted Shakespeare in a way that belied the flippant way he talked about the acting business.

When we spoke of the Bard and the current theories as to whether he or somebody else had written them, we agreed that as no royalties were being paid and everyone of the period was long gone, what was important were the plays themselves—the fact that somebody had picked up a quill, sharpened it, and wrote with the ink of the sky. Even inventing words to make his point.

When I was doing my bit for Fellini, he had my character Toby Dammit (adapted from Edgar Allen Poe's short story) doing a boozy rendering of Macbeth's speech, which climaxes with, "A tale told by an idiot full of sound and fury signifying nothing."

At the time, I assumed it was part of Fellini's own rather nihilistic take on the piece, set as it was in the hinterland after the demise of the body. Yet some months later, shooting a documentary to launch the film, we met again.

"How are you, Maestro?" I asked.

He grinned. "What has one nothing to say to another?" On reflection, I recalled a line from *The Tempest*.

"We are even stuff as dreams are made on, and our little life is rounded with a sleep."

If Shakespeare is pointing to the dream-like passing of our existence, he is inferring a Dreamer, with whom it is registering. It gave me a different take on the Macbeth line: Our endless stream of thoughts are the dream, yet when awoken to, are tales told by an idiot.

It's funny how things you experience that don't really register at the time embody themselves in your psyche, returning unbidden years later.

When I had just left home and was sharing with two other actors a basement in Harley Street, I was befriended by the manager of a small cinema in Baker Street. They frequently aired really interesting older films. I caught Laurence Olivier's Henry V there; and the manager, who often manned the box office himself, told me of a film version of *Romeo and*

Juliet with Norma Shearer, Leslie Howard, and John Barrymore. Seeing my obvious enthusiasm, he offered to get a print and screen it. Which turned out to be on a Saturday. I was as thrilled as I had been as a boy going to the Saturday morning picture shows at the Odeon Upton Park.

It has occurred to me that a lot of the names I mention that shaped my ideals will be unknown to you. If you have the time to check some of them out, you will bear witness to the timelessness of their artistry—as I did when I saw Leslie Howard's Romeo and John Barrymore's Mercutio. Both actors were at the top of their game, but I was particularly curious about Barrymore as there had been talk in the Irish side, my dad's mother, that we were related to the Drews. And, like any young actor hoping to become a member of the business will grasp at any straw, I was happy to believe it. Barrymore's rendering of the Queen Mab speech stayed with me for years, particularly that Queen Mab, the midwife of the fairies, comes in a shape no bigger than an agate stone. The dusting down of the line came again when I worked for Fellini and he told me he saw himself as a midwife when shooting a film. Could it be that Shakespeare's invention of the royal Mab be part of my own structure? Did she visit me in those moments between "action and cut"? The Mab became my Queen.

Enter Orson.

In 1967, James Fraser, my long suffering agent, the first and only professional to witness my Iago, asked me if I would like to go to Paris to meet Orson Welles. Is a maraschino cherry red?

The following evening, I arrive at the designated restaurant. As I enter the cavernous space, all painted white, my eye is drawn to the only occupant. He is sitting against the far wall, dressed in black. It is, of course, Mr. Welles. I track in to get a close up, breathing deeply to fill the space between us.

We shake hands. He indicates the chair opposite him and I sit down.

"Are you travelling alone?" I ask.

The reply rumbles toward me from under the table and over it.

"It depends."

I glance around at the table set for a lot more than two and ask, "Are a lot of people joining us?"

"It's you and me for now. But I tend to accumulate," he says with the famous grin. "You OK with red?"

A waiter has arrived with a bottle, extracts the cork and gives Orson a taste. After he pours us both a glass, he places the bottle beside me. Throughout the evening, while I was never aware of my host taking a drink, he regularly leaned over and nudged me to refill his glass, which had magically emptied itself.

He had a script from a Spanish classic called *Divine Words*, which he wanted me to read. He would get it to me. I had the impression he approved of my showing up alone. It was noticeable throughout the evening that whenever I revealed a new facet of myself, he seamlessly accommodated me and broadened his responses.

After highlighting a few of the specialities on the menu, all meat dishes, I was forced to confess I was a vegetarian. He didn't pause, and with the same enthusiasm, reeled off a few without meat. Charm is a maligned word these days, yet Orson Welles bore witness to its original meaning. It was as natural to him as song is to birds.

As the evening progressed and I became more comfortable in his presence, I asked him why he had such a hard time putting films together considering the depth of his genius and the dross that was increasingly being produced.

"The trouble began with *Kane*," he answered, "Or rather its inspiration, William Randolph Hearst—the big man with the thin but far reaching voice."

I knew what he meant. It was said that the publishing magnate's influence was so great that by use of media which he'd controlled, he had pushed the United States into war with Spain at the turn of the century. Destroying the career of a film director would have been no problem for Hearst.

According to a story I'd recently heard, Ronan O'Rahilly, the founder of Radio Caroline, had commissioned a script for Orson, with the money in place to make the film. The night before the cheque was to be signed O'Rahilly was at a dinner party with the backer. Some friends of the publishing magnate were also at the table and conversation turned to the upcoming movie and its director. Things were said and warnings issued. By morning the backer and his backing had vanished. I knew about this because one of the parts had been written with me in mind.

"Is that why you're planning to shoot this one in Spain?" I asked.

"It is where the money is. I can shoot anywhere." Again the famous smile. And then, "I'm a high wire act. I guess you are, too."

"I'd tell you if I knew what you meant."

"No safety net. Oven fresh, when you perform."

"When I'm out there. I aspire to it. Haven't cracked it on the stage though."

"You'll get there."

Encouraged by the turn of the conversation, I asked, "Any tips?"

After tapping my arm and indicating his empty glass, he considered. "The moment before you go on... assure yourself you're going to get to the end. That's what opera singers do. The more you trust in the muse, the more she'll be there for you."

"Can you tell me how *you* feel the muse?"

He smiled. "No." Another smile. "If we do the movie, we'll have lots to talk about."

I held his glance. Would I ever get another chance? "I bet you can describe her... Queen Mab."

He looked at me anew. Truly engaging me. There was a pause until, finally, he said. "It's one manifesting through the many."

His answer was in keeping with Shakespeare's intention of Queen Mab, the fairy mid-wife from Romeo and Juliet, helping sleepers give birth to their dreams.

But then, why wouldn't his answer be spot-on? Orson knew all about dreams, about their inspiration and struggle towards fulfilment.

I wanted more, but by then the room had begun to fill up and, hearing his famous voice, other diners came over to shake his hand. Some accepting his openness, sat down; an impromptu audience, at which I was a courtier. Orson had energy and time for everyone.

After Orson died, Jeanne Moreau said of Orson Welles, "He was a king without a country." To me, he was royalty whose domain was his own aura. The wonderful treatment of *Divine Words* didn't happen. He failed to raise the bread.

With the dervishes, *Cape Town*, 1974.

INTUITION

There is always a moment in the life of an artist when he is either forced or chooses to trust solely in intuition, becoming the high wire artist that Mr. Welles held in such high regard. Sacrificing rationality and understanding; this is the price the muse demands.

One of the world's greatest trumpeters died recently. Maurice Murphy was his name. Maurice Harrison Murphy—a name you may not recognize, yet his horn you would certainly have heard. He blew the principal trumpet of the opening fanfare of *Star Wars* and later on the *Superman* films, to which the whole world listened.

Mr. Murphy was a self taught virtuoso born into a coal mining family in the north of England. He started playing with a Salvation Army band when he was a boy. He grew up in the north and loved it, refusing to relocate to London until he was 41, eventually joining the London Symphony Orchestra in 1977. His very first outing with the Orchestra was the recording of the *Star Wars* soundtrack and, as principal trumpet, played the opening bars. John

Williams, the composer, later commented, "It was an electrifying moment, the whole orchestra was stunned."

One of the characteristics that set him apart was that he was never ever seen to practice. Even when his colleagues were warming up before a concert, Maurice would finish his coffee; walk straight on stage and play, whether it was "The Trumpet Shall Sound" in Handel's *Messiah* or Mahler's Fifth Symphony.

Maurice Murphy was as familiar with his horn as we actors are with our voices: he held no dreams of stardom, but to anyone who appreciates musical artistry, it's evident in his playing; the doing is the outcome.

I wouldn't mind in the least to have Gabriel blowing second trumpet to Murphy's celestial high B flat when my time comes.

* * *

Over the years, people close to me have commented on the time I spend alone. It isn't a criticism but, nevertheless, warrants comment. I seem to recall often spending time on my own. But it was only after my first big emotional upset that I realized it was easier to be alone than try to distract myself by filling the space with chums, and not being good company as a result. When I am by myself, I don't think of myself as alone. When I am on my way to a meeting, an audition, or even before "curtain up" or "action," I view myself to be gathered with a friend who will be with me always. I'm always open to take a moment to be with myself. As I have discovered, to be with myself I have to be myself.

There is a simplicity that can't be reached through effort; and any director or producer worthy of his sea salt will more than likely be on a similar wavelength and resonance. You may be the keynote in the octave he or she is looking for or your very presence the master key that unlocks the project. Nothing worse than a director who when you nail it first take, requests you to "give me one for Lloyd's." Illustrating he isn't attuned to your heart's voice, the voice of the muse, the effortless voice.

* * *

When I lived in Piccadilly, I had a neighbour who was friends with the Queen Mother. When this senior royal reached her eightieth birthday, my neighbour threw a celebratory lunch for her. It was a small gathering, including Luciano Pavarotti and one of the leading journalists and theatre critics at the time, Bernard Levin. I was invited.

These occasions with members of the royal family are always a bit ticklish. Prior to Princess Diana joining the elite group, their interactions with the public were carefully managed, including regular newspaper features, the bestowing of honours, and Royal Film Premieres.

Another princess, Margaret, preceded Princess Diana; she had tried to break the mould but had been kept in check. I met her originally in the line-up when *Far From the Madding Crowd* was premiered. The fact that we had chatted rather easily was noted by the distributors and their publicity team and, at the soiree afterwards that Princess Margaret attended, I was steered toward her as soon as I arrived. I definitely got the impression the feisty princess had been constricted by her blue blooded birthright. We soon were talking about our love lives, and I asked her how she'd made out as a young girl. She confessed that as a teenager she had often watched burly labourers fixing the road outside the palace and had fantasies about them. After that first exchange, I was warned by the publicity chief to watch myself, as apparently she had been known to lull commoners such as myself into a comfort zone and then suddenly become extremely "royal" if she felt you'd overstepped the mark. This was never my experience, however. The Princess's spontaneity wasn't at all partial and that was her charm—and a problem for the other royals.

I digress. Fleur Cowles, my neighbour, was a wealthy American socialite who gave the aforementioned birthday lunch. It was only a stroll to get to Fleur and her husband Tom's apartment. I arrived on time. Champagne was already flowing and Bernard Levin, who I knew, introduced me to Pavarotti, who I didn't.

As soon as we were seated, Bernard suggested to the table—there were a dozen or so of us—that Maestro Pavarotti sing "Happy Birthday" to the Queen Mum. The Maestro graciously accepted on the condition that we all accompany him. He tapped his glass and off we went. So I can claim to have sung with the leading tenor of the day, albeit not in the same key.

After lunch, the Royal Mother seated herself on a sofa and various guests, selected by Fleur, were brought into the Royal orbit, where we stood trying not to look as though we were in a queue. I soon spotted that she wasn't really talking to everyone; some just took her hand and moved away. When my turn came, I breathed out—thought by therapists to assuage apprehension—and sat down next to her. She looked at me, not unkindly, and stated, "You are an actor, I believe."

She used a full weight on ac-tor.

"It's true, Ma'am. Man and boy, 15 years."

"What would I have seen you in?"

It was an unusual question. Thinking to myself, if she's eighty, she probably hasn't been to the pictures lately to catch mine or anybody else's, I said, "D'you have a video?"

"I do," she said. "But I prefer to see films in the cinema. I love the moment when the lights go down."

I instantly understood. It's the unique feature of the movie theatre outing—when, from the safety of your seat, your individuality is in part merged with the collective consciousness of the audience. In fact, it was that magical moment at my very first film, in the company of my mother, which grabbed my total attention and addicted me to a life in cinema. That moment of merging before the projector rolled and the illusion of light and shadow began. That moment of losing one's self, of letting go.

She must have felt the same way.

I was suddenly at ease.

"Yes, Ma'am, that moment, I know exactly what you mean."

White tie and tails with the Queen Mum.

WHO ARE YOU?

During the eight years I was "resting" and "not wanted on location" as film extras call it; I did spend a lot of that time in India. It is, after all, the land of God-men; and while the title can be viewed as someone who points the way, in my experience, it was frequently the blind pointing the way to the blind.

Yet it is the exception that proves the rule, as they say, as it was my great good fortune to come across an exception in one of the poorer suburbs of what was then called Bombay, and is now Mumbai. Khetwadi was the district; at the time I happened upon it, one of the least privileged in the great metropolis.

On leaving the Taj Mahal, the doorman, who had hailed the taxi, asked me my destination. The doorman spoke good English; lots of the drivers didn't. When I replied, "Khetwadi," he gave me what my gran would have called an old fashioned look. Seeing my blank expression, he replied, without judgment, "It is the cat district, Sa'ib."

I don't think he meant the four-legged ones.

Maharaj, as I came to know him, resided in a small old apartment block in front of which was an open sewer. Before negotiating the best way to ford this waterway bubbling with refuse, I saw opposite a public latrine. As I had no idea what would await me inside or how long the audience would take, I decided to relieve myself before I found out. Maharaj had no telephone and I had no appointment. The stench when I entered the public lavatory was like no other I had encountered. Further investigation revealed why. The stalls were cornucopias filled to overflowing with stools of all shapes and sizes, and the stand-up urinals, battlements of a similar order. Ramparts of shit piled chest high. In spite of the overwhelming abasement of my olfactory organs, my curiosity was aroused. How had it been achieved? The customers must have been gymnasts. Leaping somersaults to take a crap!

I stepped over the creek of sewage and entered the humble dwelling, my bladder unrelieved. Once through the front door, open, was a ladder angled up into a square cut into the ceiling. On the floor at its base, several pairs of shoes. I was joined by a young woman, his daughter, who motioned me to climb the ladder. As my head went through the opening, I had a moment to see that a living space had been created by utilising the high ceiling of the original space, before a newspaper was lowered by one of the group, and my eyes were gripped by the most penetrating gaze I have ever encountered, as my face was about level with his crossed legs. I clambered up into the room, in which I couldn't straighten up. I looked around. The very thin man with the piercing eyes said something in a language I couldn't understand and motioned me to sit down. I did. Both of the older men, who had been absorbed in sections of the *Times of India*, also lowered their news sheets and one of them said in accented English, "Maharaj says make yourself comfortable and meditate."

I felt the cocoanut matting through my khadi pyjama drawstring trousers. The air in the room was filled with the smoking, burning joss sticks. It was that cheap, sweet kind—and strong—obviously, to offset the latrine opposite and the sewer below. My mind wasn't steady at all, but I reassured myself with the fact that at least I had made it. Maharaj had returned to his broadsheet. It transpired that the guru didn't speak English and was awaiting a translator, who appeared through the floor a few minutes later.

Then the inquisition began.

"Who are you?" was his first question.

"I am Terence, from England."

"Yes. But who are you?"

"Well, I'm an actor."

"Yes. But who are you?"

"I. I'm me." I started to feel like an idiot.

"Who is *me?*"

I can only gesture. Helpless.

He continues to stare at me, like a bird of prey eyeing a mouse. Finally he speaks. The translator translates. "Come back tomorrow. Eleven A.M."

The satsang is terminated. He fires up a beedi, a local cigarette made of a dry leaf rolled around a few strands of tobacco.

I touch my forehead. I feel like a serf. I thank the translator, who speaks perfect English. I compliment him. "You speak better English than me."

He smiles. "Well. I learned it. You just picked it up. See you tomorrow."

I leave the building, step over the sewer, and turn left. I get to the end of the road and see a café. I go in and order a chai. I need it. I feel I have been let out of school at the end of a long, tough first day. The chai arrives in a china cup with saucer. It is very sweet, an old fashioned taste from the blitz. I later discover they make it with condensed milk.

The axiomatic questioning continues on the second visit. Until finally I own up. I don't know who or what I am. Not really.

This momentarily satisfies him. His attention refocuses on the other listeners sitting cross-legged around the space.

One of the group, I believe he was Canadian and new like myself, asks, or rather, states, "I've heard you are a great Jnani (master) and yet you are a chain smoker."

"Who's a chain smoker?" the translator relayed.

As the dialectic of Maharaj consisted initially of bringing to our attention that we are not our bodies or our minds, it was a given that he had long since severed any identification with his.

On the last of my visits to Maharaj when he was in the final stages of throat cancer, it is worth mentioning that another would-be acolyte asked, rather brazenly, I thought, "If you are such an enlightened soul, and have a serious cancer condition, why are you still smoking?"

"Who has a serious cancer condition?" was the response.

I am getting ahead of myself. The translator, Mr. Sapre, often brought his wife to the meets and, on discovering that I was staying at the Taj, suggested to me that I invite Maharaj there for tea. He would enjoy it, she assured me.

The old section of the Taj Mahal hotel has been kept in the spirit in which it was designed. But there is a rumour quite in keeping with the continent's whimsical reputation. The hotel was designed and constructed to commemorate Queen Victoria's visit to the jewel in the crown of her empire. The architect awarded the design came to Bombay. Selected the site. Chose the finest of the country's materials. Appointed a Master Builder to oversee the project, and sailed home to Britain. On notification that the project had been completed, he booked passage to India, intending to sail into the bay of Bombay and see his masterwork from the ship as his sovereign would see it on her arrival. As the liner neared the port, with the architect standing proudly on the prow of the ship, he realized something was shockingly amiss. The Master Builder and his crew, left to their own devices, had built the hotel back to front. The architect killed himself. It doesn't do to take your eye off the ball in the construction business, in India or anywhere else.

The natives have idiosyncratic ways of making the best of a bad job. A swimming pool was designed to fit into the circular design of the front, now the back, and the rooms designed to face onto the city, which now faced the sea, were upgraded.

It was in the first floor restaurant named the Sea Lounge that I met Maharaj for tea. He arrived with Mr. and Mrs. Sapre. His usually crumpled khadi kurta and pyjama were crisp and lightly starched and he was sporting a sparky, red, short-sleeved woolly cardigan, which perfectly complimented his birth sign, Sagittarius. As he stomped up the wide, carpeted stairs toward the entrance to the Sea Lounge, grasping his long walking stick, he looked like any other Bombay walla of a certain age who hadn't bought into western gear and persisted with the traditional white cotton Khadi so perfect for the climate. Ascending the stairs, he didn't even raise a glance from passersby, and I wondered how often in my own life I had passed an individual who had been blessed—as Krishnamurti, who described the event as "the ocean was poured into the drop." Or as the fella I was taking to tea, who in answer to the enquiry about his own condition had stated, "The Universe floats within me as a cloud in the sky."

Settled around a window table with a view on the ocean was arranged quite a high tea, with a large pot of Assam's best small leaf tea, a jug of hot water and tea strainers; no tea bags at the Taj.

A fellow tourist, an American, who was also staying at the Taj, decided he would crash the party. He was by profession a "channeler," giving health tips and emotional help from an "old Chinese guide" on the other side. He didn't actually take a chair but semi-sat on the broad sill in the window and listened to what Maharaj, via Mr. Sapre, was saying.

He then asked, "Look, I am married. A very nice woman, we have two kids. She's not dumb, but she doesn't understand things the way I do. It's awkward socially. Any advice?"

Maharaj didn't pause. "Who is this I you refer to? Show him to me. If you can't, then wake up from the dream and where are the others?"

He left without touching his cup of Assam.

Mr. Sapre told me that Maharaj gave short shrift to seekers "who want to wake up while remaining comfortably asleep."

Sitting opposite Maharaj in the relaxed ambience of the grand hotel and having the sage to myself, as it were, made me at ease and I asked him some personal questions. He told me he had been a beedi roller by profession; a maker of the curious local cigarettes, and extremely low on the food train. He spoke a dialect not well thought of in the caste system and didn't consider himself promising material at all. He was invited by a friend to visit his guru. It transpired he had only seen the guru a few times and had been told "that he wasn't what he thought he was." This seemingly simple statement had resonated with him and he began to pay attention to the constant in himself, I am, the feeling of actual being. Quite soon afterward, a shift happened. Instead of observing life as in front of him, like a movie, the film was within him. Life thereafter had been lived accordingly.

I told him that some years before I had met the renowned philosopher Jiddu Krishnamurti in Rome. Had he ever met him? "No," he replied. "But we are in the same ancient state." He drank some of his tea and selected a pastry.

I had been rigorously adhering to a vegetarian regime for some years and had become increasingly preoccupied with diet; I thought, as I am in the company of a character who bore witness to wisdom, I might as well get a definitive take on the subject.

"What's your opinion about the food we eat?"

Maharaj didn't pause and Mr. Sapre translated.

"Good food. Good body."

"That's it?"

"That's it. Use your attention on the I am."

This had been his uncompromising point during the morning meetings. He returned to it continually.

"So the feeling that we have of am-ness. What you call the *I Am*, that's it?" I asked.

"The *I Am* is not it. But paying attention to it will allow a blossoming. You can't see the eye without a mirror, because it looks. Same with the *I Am*, because it is looking, yet paying attention to it helps. Will clean the glass that permits seeing clearly what is present here and now."

I opened my mouth to question further but his unwavering glance held mine. And then...

"Do you believe you came out from your father's dick?"

No more questions arose. I was aware of the sounds in the lounge, muted conversations, chinking of china cups and saucers, but a pervasive stillness filled the space that seemed to incorporate them all.

My final visit came on the last morning of my sojourn in Bombay. I arrived at eleven A.M. to find a lot of people in the ceiling room, along with a baby girl no more than two years old. Mr. Sapre wasn't in attendance, but a fellow translator was, whose English was also immaculate. He told me that Maharaj's daughter was busy and her husband was at work so the child had been left with her grandfather.

The low-ceilinged room where he lived, slept, and lectured wasn't a recent construction, although it kept its original haphazard collection of furniture and objects obviously moved from below to give it a lived-in appearance. I assumed this because in the mix of stuff I was certain Maharaj had no use for was a big ornate mirror that had been leaned against the wall in front of which was the mat that the sage sat on.

The little girl obviously thought the world of her granddad and stayed close to him. During the morning when Maharaj was expounding on the subject of what we were in actuality, the sky of present-awareness, in which all thoughts, sensations, travails, troubles, feelings negative and positive were born, shaped and passed as clouds in the unending unchanging sky, the baby girl started to climb up his arm onto his shoulder. At one point, she was actually draped over his shaved head. He wasn't distracted, but continued regardless. He seemed to me as the unquestionable sky of which he spoke.

I bade him and the translator farewell, started to climb down the ladder and stopped to take last look around the little room. The translator said to me, "Have you lost something?" Maharaj immediately interjected, "You can find what you have lost, but you cannot find what you have not lost."

I stepped out into the hot midday. I must have automatically turned left, preoccupied with the fact that in all probability I would never see him again. And, not wanting to leave his presence, the image of his unforgettable face filled my mind. Almost at the same time, a curious thing happened. As the image completed itself, it gently fragmented into squares of confetti, leaving my head empty. Everything came to a stop. I was aware only of the air entering the nostrils, the heart beating, and the feeling of being alive. Directly in my line of vision was the chai house, its previously unnoticed name: Heaven Café.

It was just after sunset when the Air India jet lifted off from the Santa Cruz Airport in downtown Bombay. The city lights twinkling below reminded me of the last time I left Japan, Kyoto to be precise. I had been camped out with a geisha in her bijou tatami hotel for two. To be frank, I felt I had died and gone to heaven until at the end of the month she handed me a crisp sheet of paper covered with Japanese calligraphy—save the bottom line, in Yankee dollars.

In my efforts to be courteous with the courtesan, as well as coughing up the staggering monthly total (worth every cent, I should add), I had mastered a few phrases of the local lingo, including a word I was partial to—*Wabi*. A description usually applied to objects, and meaning a patina of beauty added by the passage of time. The word came to mind as I pictured Maharaj; wabi indeed. It was followed, however, by the realisation that I had slipped into the extra layer of unobserved thought which prompted ninety percent of everything I said and did.

"Where was this *I* that controlled so much of my life," he'd chided me. "Could I show it to him?" I'd have to alert a deeper eye on my return to the helter-skelter of show biz, if serious about living life to the max.

Sri Nisargadatta Maharaj

DIET

Of all Tom and Ethel Stamp's kids, I was the most finicky to feed. Even after the war, when my dad returned from active service in the Merchant Navy, food and cash were scarce. Nothing was ever thrown away. All grub recycled. Today, I feel we were lucky growing up with such a maternal mother who was an exceptional cook, because although much of what we ate didn't have much nutritional substance, the tender loving care with which it was prepared probably made up for it. The efficiency of the young child's system can't be overlooked either. Even so, I had a kaleidoscope of ailments. Usually fixed by removing the symptom. My tonsils were taken at three, my appendix at twelve. Naughty organs sharply cut out. It was only at twenty-six when I was diagnosed with ulcers that I began putting my past symptoms together and realised that punishing the offending symptom may very well have been disguising the cause, driving it deeper and increasing the discomfort. Left to my own devices and the lack of the heart-warming cuisine of my mother, my digestive problems escalated.

At the start of my adventure with film director Federico Fellini in Rome, I was having intimations that abdominal pains could affect my work. Yet as they say in the East, when the pitch of the individual's cry is right, the solution appears. Fellini appointed a translator to help me get by when he wasn't around. The wonderful Patricia was also an astrologer. She advised the Maestro himself, I believe. She explained to me that far from being the culprit, the digestive system of the Cancerian archetype (me) is more like its barometer. I could, for example, refrain from eating meat and fish and see if anything changed. It did. I only intended to take it on board for three months, but after three months the condition had improved considerably. I thought, no need to rush back into roast beef. My mother, of course, thought I would die, yet accommodated the vagaries of my new diet.

On the downside, after the initial improvement, the pain in the upper gut returned. However, the slow revolution and return to organic "health" food was starting. I no longer felt so isolated. The world of healthy eating manifested in much the same way that the world of actors manifested when I began drama school.

It began to dawn on us youngsters of the Sixties that all the differing "worlds" were happening at the same time. A shift or change of vibration was the only travel ticket needed. A particular evening changed my focus. The male half of the singing duo Nina and Frederik, or Baron Frederik Van Pallandt, to give him his full due, had recently split from his wife Nina. I had helped him secure a set of chambers in the Albany.

The original house built in 1770 was sold by the Duke of York in 1802 when he was strapped for cash, for $37,000. The enterprising developers, Alexander Copeland and Henry Holland, the architect, constructed two parallel buildings that ran the full length of the spacious garden behind the original mansion, providing sixty-nine bachelor apartments, known as sets, which he sold to aristocratic chums who had sons who wanted to live in London. To my knowledge, they were the first built-to-order apartments in England. Lord Byron, Disraeli and Pitt had previously resided in them, and later, Graham Greene, Terence Rattigan, Aldous Huxley and Edward Heath, to name but a few. The covered walkway runs through the centre of the garden, giving it stillness and a sense of timelessness. Walking towards the south exit, I often imagine Piccadilly as it once was, filled with the clatter of horse-drawn carriages, while the north gate opens onto Savile Row, where Beau Brummell shopped for his threads and where, forty-two years ago, I stood and listened to the Beatles perform their final concert on the roof of the Apple Building.

In 1969, I was living in D1 on the ground floor, and Frederik two floors above in D6. The Baron was, by his own admission, something of a "short order cook," and around seven o'clock my telephone would ring, and I would be invited up the four steep flights of stairs to join him for supper. On the evening in question he had two other guests, and the menu had been put together in advance. The original invitation had been to an alternative doctor who interested Frederik, a practitioner using a "black box" that reputedly was effective even in the absence of the patient, utilising only a lock of hair. The doctor had asked to bring with him a colleague and they arrived together. He introduced his pal as Doctor Maughan. Both men were in their fifties or sixties. I must confess I don't recall a lot of the discussion. The Baron himself, the son of the leading ambassador to the Netherlands, had been schooled all over the world, finishing at the Canadian University, McGill; he was a contemporary of Leonard Cohen. I never witnessed him out of his depth, even though I frequently was.

We all sat around with our plates of food. The Baron didn't have a dining room or a dining table, so we ate from our laps.

Initially, I interpreted Dr. Maughan's demeanour as distant, as he appeared detached and didn't contribute much, while Frederik, a master storyteller, did the bulk of the talking. When we finished eating, Dr. Maughan commented on the vegetarian nature of the meal. Frederik explained that it was something I was getting into, as I was trying to cure my digestive problems.

At that point Dr. Maughan turned his attention to me.

"How's it going?" he asked.

"It varies," I responded. "Some days I'm pain free."

"How are the nights?"

"Same. Some are okay."

"What's the pain like?" he asked.

"Like a cat scratching to get out."

He took a moment, still holding my attention, then said, "Might be allergies."

It wasn't a word I had heard before in relation to food so I didn't comment. Taking in my blank face, he added, "Modern food. Modern life. The body has to play catch-up. The human digestive system hasn't noticeably altered in thousands of years. Food production has—in spades. The discomfort may be the body's way of telling you something."

This was an angle I hadn't heard in all my trips to Harley Street. It was the unadorned sense it made that resonated with me.

"How, how do I find out?" I asked.

Dr. Maughan gave his first smile of the evening. "A fellow a lot smarter than me advised, 'Physician, heal thyself.'" He paused. When he continued, his change in tone added weight to what he said. "You could put yourself on an exclusion diet. Say for a month, then introduce, re-introduce foods one at a time. Plain organic brown rice could be the staple. I believe basmati has an extra amino acid in its chain." He turned to the black box doctor, who added, "You could boil a cabbage and drink the water from it, just to be sure you're getting everything you need."

Dr. Maughan continued, "When you introduce the individual foodstuffs, you will have to wait ten minutes or so for what we call the masked intoler-ance, or masked response. As you will in effect be practising taste abstinence, your mind will be pleased with anything that is tasty. You have to wait for that to pass. Then the body will give you its verdict. So, a month of rice and cabbage water, then try a bit of cheese after a few hours, slice of bread, etc."

We later learned that Dr. Maughan was the leading light of the ancient cult of Druids. Anyway, he prompted the next stage of my food exploits, and I had reason to believe he knew more than he told me, a lot more.

His final remark to me: "Remove the cause, the effects remove themselves."

Also, his casual remark, "Have a piece of cheese and a few hours later a slice of bread," proved prophetic, as wheat and dairy (all products made using cow's milk) turned out to be the bad boys.

* * *

Many years later, my path crossed that of the eminent Professor Brostof, who held the chair at Kings College for the effects of food on health. He confirmed that one in four people in the U.K. is intolerant to either modern wheat or dairy, but few know it. It was my luck to cop for both. Initially, I felt like killing myself when I looked down the road to the rest of my life without a slice of buttered toast or a cup of sweet milky tea—comforts that since the Blitz I had turned to in tough moments.

The improvement in my health, however, was dramatic, and within weeks I became aware that any slip from the straight and narrow was paid for by the loss of well being with stomach upset or even a mouth ulcer. Wheat gave rise to digestive problems, lethargy, sometimes headaches. Dairy primarily caused respiratory complications, hay fever, multi sneezes, sinus, even asthma.

Initially, I kept the dietary changes to myself because I wasn't sure I would be able to stay with it; and then when the pain stopped and I began to experience the feeling, albeit subtle, of well being, my narcissistic element assumed the remedy for my ill health was peculiar to me. I didn't accept invitations to dine at people's homes.

Of course, when I uncovered the usual suspects (wheat and dairy) and cottoned on that, the negative results were not dose-related but idiosyncratic—the tiniest amount of either would cause a reaction within minutes—I usually asked the waiter to double-check with the chef what was actually in the dish.

These days, I tolerate and enjoy products made from sheep and goat's milk, as well as the original or ancient strains of wheat known as spelt and kamut.

Matilda and me, Farm in Ibiza.

It wasn't all work at the farm. Ibiza.

In the music room. Ibiza.

THE HIGH WIRE

Herbert Kretzmer began his life and career as a journalist in South Africa. He came into my life in 1962, arriving at the flat in Ebury Street to interview me for the *Daily Express*. He was the broadsheet's theatre critic at the time and doubled as their showbiz journalist. In fact, during his tenure in Fleet Street, he interviewed many of the notables who came to those shores, and many who didn't. We got along famously and remain friends today. He no longer works as a newspaper man. He retired when *Les Misérables* the musical, for which he wrote all the English lyrics, hit the jackpot.

In the 1950s, he spent time in Spain, and interviewed both the great matadors of the era: Antonio Ordoñez, who became close friends with Orson Welles—it is on Ordonez's ranch that Orson was laid to rest—and Luis Miguel Dominguin, the tall aristocratic Spaniard known outside the ring for his tempestuous affair with Ava Gardner, who was married to Frank Sinatra at the time.

Kretzmer talked with Dominguin on the eve of his return to the ring after a lag of many years. The maestro, who had debuted at age eleven, told him he was returning because "life was not dangerous enough," and likened fighting with bulls to making love to a beautiful woman and being discovered by her husband... with a gun! He confessed to beginning his comeback in the Balearics away from Madrid and Barcelona as "learning to love with country girls."

During his audience with Ordoñez, he asked the great man to describe the day leading up to the fight, which usually began at 6:30 in the evening. Ordonez explained that the afternoon was spent in a room at a good hotel near the plaza where the spectacle was staged. The shutters would be drawn. He would be alone with the sounds of the bands and the revellers celebrating the day of the fiesta, awaiting his team, who would come bringing his *traje de lujes*, his suit of lights—designed for him by his friend Pablo Picasso—and help him dress.

"Are you nervous?" Kretzmer asked.

"The bull isn't in the room," Ordoñez answered.

Kretzmer knew that when a matador is gored, the injury is measured by how many inches the bull's horns have entered his groin. He waited. Ordoñez continued. "Waiting in the ring, yes, there is fear. As soon as the bull sees me, no!"

I am not comparing the actor on stage or in front of a camera with the extreme courage of a matador on fight day. Yet the level of required awareness begs comparison. The bull is not in the hotel. In the ring, one's feet in the heat of the sand, the fear is the anticipation of the animal's attention, but as it charges, no. No room for fear. For the fighter of bulls, fear is thought. No space for thought. This is the bottom line. Orson knew it: Ordoñez and Dominquin are perhaps the definitive examples of his "high wire" artist.

Amo, Non Amo with Jacqueline Bisset, 1979.

BROKE

While everyone was waiting for the calamitous 1984, it came a year early for me. I found myself completely without operating cash. Borrowing bus fare to take me from my girlfriend's house in Battersea and get me back to my set in Piccadilly. I would spend the morning deciding what I could sell to score the walking around money I needed for the week.

I guess I gave off the aroma of "broke," as all the furniture, carpets and objects d'art gathered little interest. The only things in my possession, in my cellar, actually, were a few bottles of a sweet wine, a sauterne named Château D'Yquem, which I had collected when times were good. As I am practically a teetotaller, the 1969 half bottles had been in horizontal meditation for fourteen odd years, only becoming more sweet, fragrant, and golden.

I discovered plenty of takers for these half bottles of nectar—connoisseurs of the grapes that are only harvested on the years they fall wondrously foul of "the noble rot" which reduces their liquidity, transmuting them into russet-like sultanas. One sale would get me through the week. During this dry period, I ran into the lovely Mara who, with her husband, owned and ran the San Lorenzo restaurant in Beauchamp Place. Not one to mince words, she demanded, "Why haven't you been in?"

"To be honest, Mara, I'm a bit short of cash."

"So?"

"Well…"

"Come in anyway. I'll feed you 'til you get back on your feet."

Her generosity of spirit brought tears to my eyes. I recalled Fellini telling me a similar story about when he was a down and out law student in Rimini. He was later to bump into his patroness at the time she was opening her first restaurant in Rome. As he was also about to start shooting *La Dolce Vita*, he made a big show of taking his stars, Marcello and Anita, to dine at her place whenever he could. Overnight it became the legendary pasta eating spot it remains today.

It is so charming that Italians still hold their artists in high esteem. I wasn't able to repay Mara in such a high profile way, yet on those occasions when I got to take Princess Diana to lunch, often with the boy princes, Mara always had a semi-private table for us.

Broke, but getting by selling vino, I called my faithful agent James Fraser.

"What's on your desk, Jim?"

"You won't like it."

"Not a question of like. It's a question of need."

"A television, six hours from three books. Rather well written. It's for Granada so you'll be shooting in Manchester."

A newcomer to Fraser and Dunlop did the deal. I later discovered it wasn't a very good one but, as my mother used to say, beggars can't be choosers.

I had managed to devote myself to film for twenty-four years. And working for Granada, I was reminded why. Television in the eighties was more about moving lips than moving pictures.

Exhausted after a full day of dialogue on location, I was too nervous to sleep before I had committed to memory the words for the following day.

I remained exhausted for the duration of the shoot.

Being in a television series gave me an unending admiration for actors who spend their working lives in the medium. "You are all better men than I am, Gunga Din."

In the final days of the TV series, I received a call from James Fraser: Stephen Frears was about to make a film entitled *The Hit* and was interested in meeting me. I knew the name. Frears had directed a film in 1971 with Albert Finney called *Gumshoe*. I liked the film but, apparently, Mr. Frears hadn't. Or rather, he'd realised that he had a lot to learn before another foray into the world of celluloid, so he'd apprenticed himself to the BBC, where he'd spent the last thirteen years in the pressure-chamber of television.

Duca di Bagnasco, *La Creatura Divina*, 1975.

THE HIT

*T*he Hit was an original, scripted by Peter Prince. I thought it was great, a thriller in a dark comedy vein, so I met with Stephen at my apartment. We got along fine. I later heard he'd been impressed with my book-lined walls. Similar to the ones he'd envisaged for the character he was about to cast.

The Hit was basically a road movie revolving around three men—the hit man, his apprentice, and the victim. Joe Strummer, the lead man from The Clash, had been set for Myron, the apprentice, but he bottled out at the last minute and was replaced with Tim Roth, who'd done a bit of British television and a lot on the boards of the Glasgow Citizens' Repertory; his transformation to film was seamless.

John Hurt signed to play Braddock, the hit man. I couldn't have been more pleased, as I had admired him from afar for years. A consummate pro, he appeared to have no problems with any of the three mediums—stage, TV, or film.

The whole shoot was on location, the length and breadth of Spain. One of the themes woven into the text is death. My character Willie has betrayed a big gang boss in London in exchange for his freedom and a new identity, has lived for many years preparing for his inevitable assassination.

The hit man's assignment is to locate him and deliver him to the man he betrayed, who intends to execute him personally.

There is a key sequence where Willie tries to convince Braddock, his captor (John Hurt), that death is only the price of having had an individuality. In other words, he accepts his fate. To this end, Willie reads Braddock a John Donne sonnet.

A great sonnet is a test for any actor, and John Donne's are considered to be among the finest. The first hurdle is that, ideally, the sonnet should be read while sustaining the intent of the piece. I had tried to recite the 14 lines in a breath but failed. In the screenplay, Willie reads the sonnet, which he carries with him. True to my game plan of "learning the wordies" in every scenario, I committed the scene and the poem to memory.

As it was the pivotal scene between Mr. Hurt and myself, I spent much time working on it in order to be as open as possible on the night, and put in many hours the night before the scene.

Murphy's Law, or Sod's Law as we Londoners call it, prevailed. Bad weather caused the shooting of the sequence to be postponed not once but twice and only on the third try was it actually committed to film.

The other thing I should mention is that whilst a lot of directors and actors are usually happy to get it on the first take, others use the first take as a rehearsal on film. It worked against me on this shoot, as both John and Stephen are in the latter category.

On the master shot, John and I played the complete scene. It went well and the camera was being reset for the singles when I felt a delicate shift in consciousness and knew from past experience there was not actually anything I could do to prolong or strengthen this shift, if this was going to be it, my moment. I was ready.

I stayed quiet. Relaxed on my mark as the minimal changes to the light plan were carried out. We were ready. Everyone was in place.

"Stand by. Camera. Action."

In that moment, I settled into the stillness which encompasses everything, and the words seemed to flow effortlessly from it.

Then, suddenly, there were strident voices in the distance; shouts cracking the calm.

The soundman called "Cut!"

An assistant was dispatched to quiet the noise-makers.

Thoughts that were only background shadows became front and centre in my mind. Willie was gone. Terence was back. The moment passed. That feeling of utter loss beginning—

Silence.

I take a deep breath. I wait. I feel the energy of our focused crew. I offer myself to it. My thoughts slow, becoming once more static on the surface of an awareness that extends in all directions. The dialogue wells up once more. Is spoken.

An unfamiliar sensation—condition would be a more apt description—it is as if every word that comes out of the mouth is accommodated by a prepared space; airy fingers into a delicate made-to-measure doeskin glove.

The take ends. The camera stops. The soft, pervasive space becomes, once again, the canvas on which the less subtle ambience arises.

I feel no impulse to do or say anything. Yet a few of the burly technicians come close to me. One grins. One rubs my shoulder. Camera is repositioned on John. We do his single. The first take is good.

Stephen asks if he'd like another. John gives one of his lugubrious grins. "I don't think anyone will be watching me when Terence is in this mood," he concludes, including me in his eye line.

With Mum at *The Hit*, first night. 1984.

FEAR

My mother died in 1986. I was in the middle of *Legal Eagles* in New York. The grief will be familiar to anyone who loses a parent. I was not able to get back to London for the funeral so I bade my farewell by way of a letter I wrote to her. In a gesture I felt she might appreciate, I set fire to it in Central Park, opposite the New York Athletic Club where I was billeted. Even as the coil of ash fell to the ground, I felt a measure of peace; but, very soon, on the walk back across Central Park south, the memories returned, bringing the sadness with them as I relived our life together.

Into this conceptual overlay came a few dominant words, "write it down," which were repeated at intervals until I reached my monastic lodgings on the 20th floor. I found my pen, but the only paper available was the blank side of my script for the film I was working on. I turned it over and, opening it onto the back empty page, started to write.

I make no claim to literary merit. Yes, I am an avid reader, but other than a penchant for letters, post-cards and greetings at Xmas, my well doesn't exactly runneth over. On this occasion, however, I could not stop. There is usually a lot of time spent waiting about on a film set, and this one with Robert Redford and Deborah Winger was no exception.

Applying for a passport shortly after this assignment, I was tempted to fill in the question as to profession by printing: "Waiting."

When *Legal Eagles* ended, my scribbling also came to a stop. I hesitate to call it a book. It was an outpouring of memories in close, medium, and long shot that flashed across the silent screen of my mind, just long enough for me to ink them onto the page. The scribbling took the pain away, as if transferring it to another dimension. It was a therapy that got me through the movie; although, most days I felt my eyes swollen with unshed tears.

The jottings ended up bound in a book, with almost no effort on my part. In sensitive moments, horizontal in bed descending into sleep or on waking, it makes sense to me that my mum had the wherewithal, even when embarking on the big sleep herself, to give me a last present. I awaited a sign that she had arrived in a safe haven. It is said that the grief tunnel has a duration of two years, but I didn't hear from her. And then, just when I wasn't looking...

* * *

In the spring of 1986, I had occasion to think of Orson Welles again.

My pal Jimmy Fraser, who had unearthed me at drama school over twenty-five years earlier, retired. I moved agencies. The new team weren't yet familiar with my anomalies, and I was in the habit of dropping into their offices just across the road in Soho. If you don't work regularly, "out of sight" is often "out of mind," even if your representation is good.

On one such visit, I was in the agency when the phone rang—actually in the office of an assistant to whom I was chatting. It was an enquiry about my availability. She relayed the details to me as she heard them down the line. There was to be a tribute to Leonard Bernstein. A fortnight at the Barbican with the London Symphony Orchestra, to include an array of his compositions, plus a rarely performed work by his early musical guru, Marc Blitzstein, the Airborne Symphony, which had not been performed since 1946 in New York. The conductor would be John Mauceri. The full London Symphony Orchestra, opera stars flown in, and a choir would participate. Maestro Leonard would be in attendance. The symphony included a narration, the speaking part they hoped I would consider, originally spoken by Orson

Welles. It was relayed to me as though I would find the fact inspiring. It had the opposite effect.

Frankly, every new facet relayed to me extended my fear threshold, until it reached critical mass.

Over the years earning my living, I had been compelled to address the fear factor on more than one occasion. The solution I arrived at was to ask myself, "What are the facts here?"

As I was hearing about the narration of the Airborne Symphony, I had the realization that the near nausea I was experiencing was out of all proportion to the gig on offer.

"I'll do it," I heard a voice curiously like my own responding. "Get the details."

I stumbled out into Wardour Street and made an escape before my resolve weakened, gulping in air to stop myself from throwing up.

There is often in the arc of a part a click. A keynote that sets the octave for the performance: a pair of shoes that gives the character purchase, a second-hand suit in a thrift store that misfits just right. In this case, the click came in the shape of a bow tie.

Since my first Royal Premiere in 1962, I have always felt comfortable in white tie and tails. In spite of the tailor Doug Hayward, and Dimmi Major, the guy who cut it, coming to my flat to show me how to wear it properly, once I was in it, everything had gone well. Which usually happens when I feel comfortably dressed. So when the Barbican production team asked me what I would prefer to wear, I requested tails. They agreed, even though it meant everyone would have to dress the same. What the hell? Wasn't it in honour of the great Leonard Bernstein?

On the other side of Piccadilly where I was living at the time, in the mouth of the small arcade opposite the Royal Academy, is one of the finest men's outfitters in St. James. Budd is the shop's name. As soon as I relocated to London's West End from London's East End, I had reconnoitred the village and sampled the best bespoke the capital had to offer. George Cleverley, who made Rudolph Valentino's button-up boots for *Blood and Sand* (he had a thank you letter to prove it) shod my idol Gary Cooper, and invented initialled velvet slippers for Winston Churchill, became my shoemaker. Budd made my linen shirts whenever they got their hands on some good stuff; the colours were limited, but I stayed with them until I discovered a Roman shirt maker who took his own dyes to the old country, where they dyed the Irish linen to order. My future ex-wife once remarked to my tailor, "He knows more about clothes than acting." If she had known of the event I am about to relate, her remark would have been more perceptive than flippant.

On the morning in question, young Rollie was on the floor. I explained to him that my tails still fitted but I needed a fresh wing collar. He enquired what I would be doing and I told him. He suggested two objects, the first a period white tie. Unlike the modern variety, it wasn't bow shaped but straight and, whilst it had to be knotted perfectly, drooped elegantly in the style of the Thirties. As the symphony was about the history of flight, culminating with the outbreak of World War Two, he felt it would be appropriate. I agreed. The second-hand tie he gave me for a couple of quid. This was the key note that set the tone of my performance. Yet it was his second brainwave that was to have even deeper ramifications.

One of the problems with the white tie outfit is that the detached stiff collar needs two studs to fix it in place, one back and one front. The back can be visualized as two brass spheres. The outer one is smaller and hinged so that it slides easily through the shirt band and starched collar before it is clicked into its holding position. The front stud is a different design. The base is a round sphere, but the end that holds both collar bands of the shirt and both ends of the winged collar is torpedo shaped for easy penetration through all four layers of material. This design can be seen as a miniature brass capstan no bigger than a fingernail. The whole contraption is covered and further secured when the bow is tied in place. Tying a bow was never a problem for me. It was a knack one learned at drama school, as actors in comedies of manners were frequently called upon to tie a bowtie as part of the action, often without a mirror. It was akin to serving tea in china cups without rattling the props.

Mr. Rollie displayed what was the modern generation of the front collar stud. Instead of the capstan design, it sported two spheres similar to the back stud, but the front, hinged part was the same size as its base button. I saw the sense of it instantly. It would feel more secure. I pocketed my purchases and left.

When I address a job, I try to keep it real, dealing with problems whether they be actual or in the mind. The first thing I looked at was redoing a work in Orson's great shadow. The fact was that no one in the audience would have seen his rendition, save Mr. Bernstein himself, maybe. That knowledge alone gave me some relief.

I decided to prepare what could be prepared, allay my misgivings about my work, and trust something would happen in the alchemy of the night. I spoke to John Mauceri on the telephone from New York.

"Don't worry," he reassured me. "I will be in London for the rehearsals."

"Rehearsals. When?"

"We have two days, one with the orchestra. Plenty of time."

Plenty of time. A day?

"I don't read music, Maestro," I confessed.

"No problem. I'll bring you in."

"Could you get me something to listen to? Where the narrator speaks. Preferably, not Mr. Welles."

"Yes. Yeah. I'll get a tape sent. See you in two weeks."

He was as good as his word. I received the tape. It wasn't Orson, thank you, God. A girlfriend of mine lent me her portable tape machine and earphones. It became my constant companion. I ran into Prince Andrew in the Burlington Arcade.

"What music you listening to, Terence?" he asked.

I removed an earpiece.

"Learning my words, Your Highness," I replied.

"What a good idea."

It was. I don't think I have known my wordies so well since my Iago days.

I also enlisted the help of my pal Nickolas Grace. Nick, or "Amazing," as I call him, is one of those undiscovered, for the most part, genii that frequent the showbiz industry in Britain. You may have caught his performance as Anthony Blanche in the original TV version of Evelyn Waugh's *Brideshead Revisited*. He was the character who stuttered so memorably. Nick is the first person I turn to for anything regarding voice or movement. His advice is always of the highest order.

We appeared together in the West End version of Bram Stoker's *Dracula*, where the critics had been intent on driving a stake through the heart of Terence, but… "It's a bad wind that blows no one any good," as my Granny Kate used to say.

Nick had plenty of experience with orchestras. He'd sung leads in Gilbert and Sullivan and also several versions of Bernstein's masterpiece, *Candide*. He told me everyone uses microphones these days. Even the rawest of screamers were miked to the max. Educated voices were the minority.

"You'll only need a minute with the mike and the sound engineer—on the day."

I owned up that I'd had virtually no radio offers or voice jobs that other actors supplement their incomes with, despite the fact that I had worked on the breath from every angle east and west most days of my working life. And, as I was in the habit of preparing my roles vocally along with everything else, I had the idea that a dialect of English from a bygone age would be fitting. I likened what I was looking for to the voices that I had listened to with my mother on the wireless during the blackout of the Blitz.

I gave him a sample of some of the narrator's lines.

"Are you learning it or reading it?" he wanted to know.

"I don't like it when I am in the audience and a performer reads his lines. There's no eye contact, less empathy."

"So. You're learning them?"

"Yeah. That's the idea, anyway. I've been working on it a lot."

"Good. Better." He paused. "You know your delivery is perfect RP (received pronunciation). You've managed it without sacrificing the essence of your voice. In fact, all you need to create that wartime delivery is to lean on the 'i' vowel. Yeah. That's what you should do—give the 'i' full weight."

He pronounced, "Evil... the algebra of pure evil."

It was extremely easy for Amazing. I grimaced.

"Look," he said. "It's extra work, a challenge. Go through the text, underline all the 'i' vowels. Evil is good because it is followed immediately by an 'l,' which you sometimes get lazy with. So, no dark 'l's for Lenny. Hey. You taught me about increasing the need."

His outings at Sadler's Wells had made him no stranger to staying on the beat.

During the last week before rehearsals, some of my family remarked it was a pity Ethel wasn't around to see this concert. My mother had played piano by ear, the life and soul of the party. None of her offspring inherited her musical gift, another reason she would have appreciated an outing to the Barbican.

My chum Hester, who'd lent me her portable tape player, had been at Ethel's bedside during her final days at the Middlesex Hospital. She was my representative amidst the family in my absence and, now, she would take my mother's seat at the concert.

Maestro Mauceri arrived. We met. We rehearsed south of the river. He brought me in as promised, once. That evening, my chum Hester made me supper at her place. She asked me if I wanted her to take me through my lines, but I felt it was time I trusted my memory. I had done enough. In those days, I was living the food-combining regime, no protein with carbohydrates. That evening, we had salad and rice. During the meal, she commented on the length of my nails.

"Males shouldn't have long nails; it's effeminate," was what she actually said—before setting to work trimming mine.

The Pope has a funny hat. *Vatican Conspiracy*, 1982.

VANITY

The day dawned. I awoke in the 10½ tatami room that I had constructed for myself on the top floor of my chambers, inspired as I was after my sojourn in Kyoto. The early April light was glowing through the shoji paper windows. I usually take it easy during the day of a first night. I stretched out on the futon and planned the day backwards, starting from my arrival at the Barbican scheduled for 6:30. I decided to spend some time at the steam baths, like one of my early heroes, Socrates.

I got up and extracted my tails from their cover. Placed my Chinese cherry red amber links and studs halfway through the starchy cuffs and front of the dress shirt. Took the trees out of my black patent shoes and slipped a pair of black silk socks inside them, before putting them back inside the travelling bag that I would carry on the Underground to the Barbican Centre.

Then, I shaved, knees bent, a ritual I had gleaned from a one-hour training session with martial arts master Steve Morris. Obviously sussing my pugilistic abilities within seconds, he did not teach me to fight, but graced me with something far more practical.

"Strengthens the legs while keeping the knees supple."

In my way of thinking, if in the presence of the greats you expect diamonds but get offered rubies, pick 'em up.

No weak knees tonight... I hoped.

* * *

I strolled across the three adjoining parks, only walking across grass, to get to the Queensway Turkish Baths. Halfway across Hyde Park, a large dog detached itself from its owner and bounded over to say hello, only leaving my side when its exasperated master bellowed for it to return. A good omen, I thought.

I leave for the Barbican at 5:45, carrying my performance clothes and "treading on reality at every step" as they say in Zen enclaves. By 6:30, I have arrived at my destination. Hung up my outfit in my designated dressing room, itself rather like a monk's cell. Been shown the place where I will sit when not speaking and the microphone when I do. This is a first for me. "Hello Mike."

I wave to the sound engineer in the box and give him a level. "To be or not to be, a very interesting question."

Return to my ascetic quarters: practically every surface is carpeted. There are no sharp edges anywhere for a neurotic performer to do himself harm. Perform some light breath work, tongue and voice warm up.

At 7:15, I begin to leisurely don my white tie and tails. I am still "on reality of every step" when I attempt to affix my detached collar. The back stud is easy as I had put it together before I put the shirt on. The front presents me with a problem. The amber studs in the shirt and waistcoat are in place, but when I attempt to affix the collar itself, only the two starched button holes of the shirt and one button hole of the collar are accommodated by the newly designed hinged stud. It won't take what is in fact the fourth layer of material. Try as I might, I cannot wrest the second wing of the collar sufficiently over the button to grip the hinge and make it secure. My denuded *masculine* fingertips are no help whatsoever. I look around the austere room for a tool, a sharp edge, anything. Nothing.

I hear the orchestra tuning up. I look again around the room. Take my shoes from their bags. Slide on my socks. Pull on my shoes, lace them up. Look again at the wayward flying collar in the mirror. Sharp taps on the door! "Five minutes, Terence."

A moment of panic followed by a familiar aroma; so faint I almost miss it. Gone before the thought comes. What was that smell? I know it but, no—gone. I realise I am still standing in front of the mirror, which is super glued to the wall, like everything else. The image that confronts me is lost, helpless. Then several things happen almost at once.

A third cannonade of knocks on my door and, "Overture and beginners, Sir!"

That waft of aroma again. I remember; it is the smell that greeted us on entering the provision store in the town of Yalding when we were hop-picking. It is unique and unmistakeable, giant wedges of cheese, freshly baked loaves, spam, bacon, homemade jam, pickles, everything wholesome, unwrapped, on the deep counters of a country store. Yet, how strange is that.

And then an idea slams in. I am a lefty in a right handed world. Maybe the collar and stud has a right hand bias. I reverse my hands, still impotently holding the collar and stud. It happens. It's through. It clicks.

"We are ready, Sir!"

I deftly tie the white bow. It settles first time.

There's that aroma again, more distinct, it ushers the thought of Ethel to mind.

"I get it, Mum. If you're here, you're welcome!"

I am through the door. First, up the stairs two at a time. Find my place in front of the microphone. Under my breath, "Okay, Mike, let's do it."

I had committed my lines thoroughly to memory, yet the most effort had gone into the opening salvo. If the proscenium arch collapses, my first lines won't desert me. They don't. I hear them, magnified by the electronics, reverberating around the one thousand, nine hundred and forty-nine seats of the auditorium. And then it happens, the quiet, an almost imperceptible shift: the air in the immediate vicinity of my nostrils becomes duvet soft. The centre of my being is expanding; a heightened sensitivity that takes in the whole room. It could also be an inrush of the energy in the auditorium that my consciousness, aware of its own mirror-like quality is spontaneously reflecting.

The thought arrives. Yes, there is thought, yet no thinker.

Question: What to do?

Immediately, I have a mental picture of a clasped hand concealing a thumb. What's concealed? If the hand is spread, it is empty. If kept closed, there may be something in it. No one knows for sure.

Answer: Nothing.

The words continue their flow. The action continues, yet there is no "one" acting. Thoughts arise without a thinker. There is only the seamless interaction of sound and listening.

Midpoint is traversed. My practised line: "The algebra of pure evil."

From somewhere, I hear the weighted "i," the undark "l." Perfect. I congratulate myself. My mind is working. I'm thinking. Boy, that sounded good!

Silence. The orchestra has stopped.

"Somebody's forgot a cue," I say to myself.

I glance about me. John Mauceri is staring directly at me, his baton raised.

Oh, my god! It's me!

His baton begins its downward swing.

"It begins!" I just manage to squeeze the words in under its arc.

The background of abundance shining and full, shrivelled, gone as lonely Terence steps backward, slumps onto his chair, winded. Thoughts overwhelm me.

The symphony continues. Vanity, thy name is Stamp.

What to do? Pull yourself together. Or make a start at least. I bow my head and look at my shiny black shoes. Let's put the energy in the feet. How do the feet feel? I wrinkle my toes. How is the stage actively feeling tonight? Now. Just now.

A moment before my next cue, I stand and step back into the fray. As I begin, it returns, the shift, the peaceful energy—the background always there, rarely noticed.

The symphony ends. Heartfelt applause. We all gather backstage: "Us happy few." Maestro Bernstein enters, with much aplomb. He sees me and extends his arms. We meet halfway. He encircles me in his hug. Places his mouth close to my ear and whispers, "You missed a cue."

His words reverberate.

My chum Hester has driven to the performance in her BMW. She drives me home. We park in the forecourt at Albany. She switches off the car and sits facing the Georgian mansion. The headlights of passing traffic in Piccadilly illuminate auburn shafts of her hair.

"What happened?" she asks.

"When?"

"When you dried. When you sat down, dropped your head."

"Oh. I lost the flow. Just trying to get myself together. Why do you ask?"

"I saw your mother's face, on yours. I blinked. And it vanished."

I could not answer. There is too much and nothing to say.

The next day the agency rings. "We've had an ad executive on the blower. Wants to try your... expensive voice for the new Peugeot campaign."

Is this coincidence? My mother? Or proof of Oneness?

Dancing the tango, *Prince of Shadows*,
directed by Pilar Miró.

A TRIP HOME

Shortly after the eventful happenings at the Barbican and my portrayal of The Monitor in the Airborne Symphony, Michael Cimino was reputedly in London casting around for his production of *The Sicilian*. It was the gossip of the acting community. I heard from two guys that it was mayhem in the offices where he was seeing people, as he frequently got into lengthy discussions, causing a build-up of tried and tested actors who could do nothing but wait and talk amongst themselves. One told me it was like a meat market.

My eight-year sabbatical following *The Mind of Mr. Soames* in 1969 had more than erased any ideas I had of behaving like a leading man again; still, despite a great respect for Mr. Cimino, I didn't feel ready to join a queue.

Time passed, I didn't push it one way or the other with my agents, and more or less forgot about any chance I might have had with *The Sicilian*.

Until, one morning, while seated in Fortnum and Mason's Soda Fountain at the same table that my mother and I often used to take our afternoon tea, Michael Stevenson entered my life.

Michael Stevenson is something of a legend in the film game. There is not much—or anyone—he doesn't know. And while his resume lists his array of skills—among them, line producer, co-producer, third assistant, second assistant, first assistant, personal assistant—most will know him as the finest second assistant in the business, bar none. This is his chosen role. He is frequently bought off films in production and sequestered onto others that perhaps have a difficult star.

Mr. Stevenson loves actors and they love him. He is a gentle man in the real sense of the word. All the more impressive as his gentleness is born of strength. He claims to have taken after his mother, and it isn't well known outside of East London circles that his father was John Stevenson (or Tiger Stevenson, which was the name he fought under), one of the very last pugilists to fight in the bare knuckle ring. One of his last bouts was at the Hoxton Town Hall against the fearsome father of Ronnie and Reggie Kray. This contest was called a draw after 50 or so punishing rounds. After the fight was stopped, the two combatants continued their fisticuffs in the street, to the delight of the home-going crowd. A rematch at the famous venue Blackfriars was scheduled, yet never fought, as bare knuckle fighting was outlawed. A famous pub now occupies the bloodstained site. Tiger lived to be 93 and, when in his eighties, five youths tried to push past him as he was getting off a number 9 Routemaster and took exception to the old age pensioner standing his ground. They set about teaching him a lesson. He knocked out four and the fifth ran away.

His son Michael had been in the film game almost as long as myself. He was always the first of the crew on board whenever David Lean or Stanley Kubrick began a film, as his knowledge of artists and technicians is encyclopaedic.

It was late in April, and I was in the Soda Fountain, trying to write a sequel to my first book, *Stamp Album*. A quiet morning and I had the place almost to myself, when Michael came in.

He introduced himself and then his colleagues: Cimino, and Joanna, his producer. After I had assured them they weren't disturbing me, they sat down.

I later learned they had seen most of the actors in town and were on their way to Heathrow in a black cab when Cimino asked the other Michael if there were any actors of note they hadn't seen. He mentioned me and informed them he might know a place on route to the airport where I could be found. And so it was I wound up in Sicily a month later, playing a prince.

Michael Stevenson met my late flight into Sicily himself—a thirty-mile drive. He'd have no strange non-English speaking driver holding a board for Mr. Stump, not on a Michael Stevenson shoot.

On the lengthy ride to the location, Michael explained to me that Cimino encouraged his cast to really get into their parts and billeted them accordingly. Actors playing mafia fraternized with mafia; actors playing police hung out with policemen. As I was Prince Borsa, he wanted me to stay in the best hotels and had fixed it for me to meet up with some local Sicilian aristocrats. However, the producer who had contracted me for the whole shoot balked at paying so much in the way of expenses, so Cimino paid for my stay out of his own pocket.

During my first day on set, real people were, for the most part, extras. In Sicily, no one is ever identified as mafia, and when the aristocrats arrived for hair and make-up, the Countess, whose father had been the model for my part, addressed me as Prince Borsa. Then, turning to face the others in the room, she exclaimed, "Oh, you must be playing the Mafioso!"

Most of the long hauls from location to location were overland, and the longest of the shoot was when we travelled to Agrigento. The trip took most of the day. When we arrived, the transport manager met our car and explained to me that contrary to the director's wishes, the hotel outside which we were standing was all he could get for me at present. He said he was still looking, but the town was a tourist site as it boasted an almost complete temple, built by the ancient Greeks, and good rooms were hard to find.

The hotel was tacky, especially after the luxury to which I had become accustomed. But as my chum Baron Frederik said on more than one occasion, "Aristocrats and working class can turn their hands to anything, even if it entails unblocking a lavatory."

With this in mind, I lay down on the grimy candlewick bedspread that covered the narrow bed and tried to relax, but the window was open and the screams from the pool directly beneath it were non-stop; it was obviously a stopover for tour buses. Late afternoon, it was too early for supper, too late for a nap. Besides, there was no chance of falling asleep with the racket outside from the kids' impromptu swim competition—or so I thought.

Film shoots, especially on location, are always tough, and before long I felt very weary and laid my head back against the lumpy pillow.

* * *

In 1942, when Mum and I moved from my gran's house, spacious on a wide road, with a garden and a cellar, I took an instant dislike to the downsizing. It was a two-up two-down, a scullery (a small room with a single sink), no bathroom, an outdoor loo and a small yard in which nothing ever grew. To make matters worse, unbearable sometimes, a low wooden fence separated it from the most scrumptious garden I had ever seen. While ours could be measured in feet, our neighbour's house could only be glimpsed beyond the lawns, shrubs, climbing roses, and pear trees only an arm's reach from our grasp—conference pears whose rusty skins ripened and dropped unnoticed every autumn. Except by us, of course. Held in check by a low-slung plank fence we were strictly forbidden to straddle.

The only room in 124 Chadwin Road that I genuinely liked was our bedroom, which looked out on the street. It also overlooked the only other feature I approved of—our front step, a design of square tiles, red, black, and beige. It fell to me to keep them clean, snow, rain, or sun. When Mum fell pregnant with our sister, the longed for daughter to add to the trio of sons, a new anteroom was constructed by my father Tom at one side of their bedroom—which was larger—into which we boys were relocated. I hated it.

The bizarre thing about Chadwin Road, which I was happy to abandon in my haste to move "up West," was that I periodically dreamed of returning there. These dreams took on an importance when they began to feature regularly in my adult life. When my mother's mum died, my beloved Granny Perrott, and she was finding her life a bit too much to bear, Granny Perrott would invariably manifest in her dreams. Whilst she wouldn't remember any specifics, she always woke up revived and feeling empowered anew.

My dreams, the sensible ones, had a decal. They always began with me standing on the front step looking down at the harlequin design I had taken care of as a boy. Once I entered the front door I could be anywhere, yet the dreams always opened on the red, black, and biscuit tiles.

* * *

And so it happens in Agrigento. No sooner have I closed my eyes than am once again outside 124 looking down at the adorned doorstep. I knock on the windows of the front door. They're covered in the jolly Christmas paper we had stuck on them one winter. We'd left it on as it made our front door windows resemble stained glass. No one answers. *This is not right. I have to get in.* Knock again. No answer. Momentarily, I'm stumped. Then I decide to walk around the corner, maybe to visit the local park, Beckton Park, where it is said seven winds blow.

I turn right, right again. Take the third turning into the main road, walking along the pavement opposite the park with its lido and old plane trees.

I pass number 353; a curtain in the front window moves, catching my side vision. I turn. The curtain is held back, revealing my mother. She beckons me. I walk to the front door, which she opens. I enter. "What are you doing? It's not our house."

She's walking ahead of me. She turns and smiles. I follow her, out into the garden. It is as I remember it but more splendid. I haven't ever seen it from here. I smell scented flowers, lilac. The grass and leaves are silvery. The Straffons' privet tree is in bloom, the aroma heavy. She walks ahead, with me right behind her. I see our house; the wooden fence is gone and the splendour has spilled over into our yard. "This is all ours, now," she explains.

We enter the scullery door. Speaking as she leads me up the narrow steep staircase. It is dark, as always. "I know you didn't like the back bedroom, but I want to show it to you."

We are inside the bedroom, which now has as its view the combined grounds, fruit trees and all.

In the fashion of dreams, all the family is suddenly in the room. We all look out of the window. Yet I sense danger. Carefully, I lead everybody back to the ground floor. I am right. The whole bedroom is collapsing.

My mother is unperturbed. She assures me. "Don't worry. Things are simple to fix here. Come look!" She rolls back a carpet from the floor in the middle of the living room, the same carpet that I spent hours laying on in front of the fire. I grew in a horizontal position. My father called me "the horizontal champ."

She raises a trap door in the floor that I never knew existed. It has delicate piano hinges.

She invites me closer. I see a wooden slide, like in a playground, incredibly smooth, a fine yellow wood. She urges me to inspect the space. I slip down it into a small room that is awash with glowing tribal carpets, woven from muted colours. Her voice becomes softer, conspiratorial. I can no longer see her, yet her welcoming words are close to my ear. "I made it for you. So you know you always have a place. A home. It will always be here for you. Wherever you are. Your real home."

I lay on the carpets, in the position I laid in as a youth in front of the fire. I feel I'm rising, almost levitating on a horizontal plane. Hear the tweeting of birds. Sense the dream landscape has faded.

I am back in the hotel on the candlewick bedspread. The shouts of enthusiasm and splashing have stopped. I can hear birds close by. I open my eyes. I am looking at the open windows. Near the corner of the outside mantel is affixed a nest, from the top of which I see tiny beaks. It is these from which the chirping is emanating. A swallow flies in with its beak full; it apportions its haul into the babies' open mouths. How did I not see this before?

The telephone is ringing. I pick it up. It's the film's transport manager. "Hi, Terence, I have found you a nicer hotel. I am organising transport. Come down in ten minutes."

The new digs are wonderful, with a generous ground floor room and tall doors opening onto a terrace, which itself has a view of the ancient acropolis.

I am out of the grief tunnel. My mother has landed somewhere.

You are probably wondering what I made of the timely dream. And I promise I will tell you what I think—yet not now. Later, when my mind is less fragmented by jetlag. When the muse pays her next visit.

Prince Borsa, *The Sicilian*, 1987.

PRISCILLA, QUEEN OF THE DESERT

Caroline Bliss is an actress. We met in Manchester in 1984. It can be a complicated process, friendship between performing artists. Usually, only staying in the business ensures that paths cross.

Yet it proved easy with Caroline. Shortly after we met she landed a part in the West End, and Albany, where I was living at the time was directly on her flight path to the Comedy Theatre, which she reported to six days a week. In between shows on Wednesdays we'd have a cuppa. At one such tea break she commented how harmonious my apartment was. As she is a very smart girl, I waited for the other shoe to drop, which it duly did.

"I can see why you don't go out much..."

I did my best to smile encouragingly.

"Of course, when you were working regularly, you naturally put yourself about, but nowadays nobody seems to see you. Everyone I meet who knows I know you is curious."

"Really."

"Most think you're a recluse. Of course, I'm happy to lie on your behalf…"

"So, you think I am a recluse?"

"Well, hardly anyone gets to see you these days."

"Except you."

"I'm pushy."

"I invited you to tea."

"And very good it is, too."

I was serving an organic white from the right side of the hill.

"Listen, Caroline, as we are fellow Cancerians, you can cut to the chase; otherwise, you'll be late for the half and I'll have to wait 'til next week for the pay off."

She luxuriated in the needlepoint Berger armchair it had taken my chum Silvana Mangano three years to complete.

"You should work more."

"Easier said than done. I don't like to do crap unless I haven't got the rent."

"Yes. Sure. But you've manipulated your agent to such a degree, she probably doesn't even show you most of the offers that come in."

"I don't think that's true."

"It's easy to check. Tell the agency you want to read more. Better. Tell them you want to do comedies—to look for comedic subjects."

Caroline was not someone whose opinion I took lightly.

"I can do that."

"Promise?"

"Promise."

On reflection, a lot of what she had said did resonate with me. I had put a lot of restrictions on the team: No long runs in the theatre. No TV. No first time directors. No films being shot in Australia (I'd had a really horrible time with the paparazzi and Melbourne matrons on my first trip in '66, accompanying a girlfriend to the Melbourne Cup).

I decided to take my agent out to lunch in order to fulfil my promise to Caroline.

The agency at the time was north of Oxford Street and comprised of three floors above a shop. I pressed the doorbell, announced myself and was buzzed in. My destination being the top floor, I set about climbing the steep stairs. But on the first floor landing, the partner agent, Stephanie Randall, who'd obviously overheard my well produced announcement, opened her office door, brandishing a rolled up script like a tennis racquet (she is a member of the All England Lawn Tennis and Croquet Club) and proclaimed: "This has just arrived. It's a comedy. About drag queens."

I looked about me as though someone within earshot had blown my intention.

"D'you want me to give it the once-over or d'you want to read it?" she continued.

It was beyond coincidence. I hadn't even let on about my tentative change of outlook.

"I'll read it. Thanks, Steph."

I didn't. It wasn't from lack of trying. Yet every time I opened the script, usually sat on my bespoke untreated hide settee, I only ever managed to scan a few pages before being overcome by an irresistible fatigue, which I inevitably succumbed to.

Days passed. Wednesday rolled around. In between shows at the Comedy Theatre, Miss Bliss arrived for our picnic. I had been the recipient of some small leaf Tarry Souchong mailed by a friend and was keen to hear what my fellow tea aficionado made of it.

Pointing her to her favourite chair, I pottered off into the kitchen to get started on the ritual, paying little regard to the screenplay on the circular Chinese table, where I intended to serve the new brew.

Minutes later I do.

While Caroline poured, the telephone rang.

I answered. It was Steph, from the agency. "Hello, Darling. I was wondering if you'd had a chance to look at that screenplay?"

I should mention that Stephanie Randall was trained by the great voice teacher Rudi Shelley at the Bristol Old Vic School in the Sixties; he had all his pupils "speak up" (meaning, loudly) whenever possible.

"Yes. Yes. I have looked at it." Not untrue. I had looked at it. I just hadn't managed to finish it.

"What d'you think?"

"Well. It's a bit of a one-joke piece, isn't it? 'Cocks in frocks.'"

Caroline had carefully placed her bowl of tea back on the tray and was looking in my direction.

"Oh," said the big voice on the telephone. "*We* all rather liked it."

At the time, there was only one male employed at the agency and he handled the accounts. So the "we" was a rather loaded plural. The significance of which was not lost on me, yet my attention was divided as the guest in my direct line of vision was obviously trying to get my attention, her remarks overlapping Stephanie's.

"Say yes. And hang up," was all I heard.

"What?" I asked.

"Sorry, darling, is somebody there?" said Stephanie.

"No. No, it's okay, Steph."

"Say yes and hang up," Caroline repeated with increased intent.

Stephanie, apparently hearing a feminine voice in the room, "Terence, look, if this is a bad time..."

"No. No."

"Tell her yes. And hang up."

Appearing contrite, but actually confused, I said into the telephone, "Listen, Steph. Why don't we... er... progress it. If you all like it..."

I can tell by the less strident response that my agent felt she had compromised me into a position I wouldn't normally take.

"Oh, darling, he's not very experienced, the director. It's very low budget, no money to speak of and... it shoots in... Australia."

"Progress it, Steph. Talk to you soon."

I hung up and focused my scrutiny on Miss Bliss.

"What?"

She pointed to the script next to the tea, which she'd obviously had a sneaky peak at while I was in the kitchen.

"It's a drag film, three queens in a bus going across the outback," I said.

Caroline doesn't scoff, but if she did her reaction would be close.

"What?" I challenged.

She took a moment as the aroma of the smoky tea wafted across the room.

"Your reaction is what is interesting."

"My reaction?"

"Yes. Or to put it bluntly... your fear is out of proportion to the project."

I was about to take her up on that when I recalled the sleepiness I had felt every time I tried to get through the piece.

165

"It's your reaction you should be looking at," she said.

I kept my mouth shut. She continued.

"It's simple really. Just keep saying 'yes.' Probably it will go away. Then fine. If it doesn't, somewhere along the line what is so frightening will become clear and you can address it. Do you understand? It's not a career move; it's a growth move."

She then devoted herself to her tea.

Which is more or less what happened. I kept on taking deep in breaths and letting out shallow quavering "yeses" while Caroline provided me with unyielding support. Discovering esoteric groups that provided shelter wherein individuals were encouraged to practice life in symmetry with the motions of their hearts. And, finally, expeditions to shoe stores that catered for the more sizeable of women.

On entering the first of these, the salesman had asked us what size we needed. Caroline had looked at me. I had said to her, "eleven." "Eleven," she repeated.

"We don't do small sizes,' the salesman responded.

"They're for him!" she said.

She also reported for tea with make-up and loose dresses so I could get used to the look and feel in private.

Bernadette; *Priscilla, Queen of the Desert*, 1994.

BERNADETTE

I, Bernadette, find myself standing on top of a high narrow pub bar in a mined-out mining town down under named Broken Hill—waiting to lead my fellow drag queens into an alternative rendering of "Shake Your Groove Thing."

I am conscious of the steamroller of mindless vapourings running through my brain. *"What are you doing here? You're a middle-aged man. You were the benchmark Iago of Webber Douglas. The best dressed man in England. You're a closet philosopher. You've sat with wise men. You're..."*

"Camera. Playback. ACTION!"

The intro of "Shake Your Groove Thing" blares over the sound system. DA-DA-DA-DA-DI-DA-DA.

My mind stops. I sense my lips moving, syncing the blaring words, my body gyrating—

Like I have stepped out of time. Suddenly, "Cut! Print!"

The take is over. We've done it.

Fear? Yes, there was plenty of fear, a kaleidoscope of projections of being made to look nakedly silly. It was my core dread and, ironically, that was exactly what the role demanded.

"Next Setup," I hear the director say.

And me? I'm silent, unmoving, existing in that place one finds when dread is faced and fear temporarily banished. I'd like to stay here but I know I can't.

* * *

The Australia I experienced was indeed another country from the one abandoned in the Sixties. The troupe and fellow artists were first class. It wouldn't be a fib to say I could never have pulled *Priscilla* off without Hugo Weaving, Guy Pearce and the rest of the team.

The initial days were light for me, and the transition from costume, wig fittings, and choreography went smoothly. Of course, the director had Hugo, Guy, and me out on the town in full drag, an interesting sight. On leaving my hotel to meet at Hugo's house to get dressed and made up, I said to the night manager, "I may look different when I come back—feminine. It's for a movie."

"They all say that," she retorted.

What I hadn't paid enough attention to was the virtually impossible task of performing in a synchronised dance trio while simultaneously keeping perfect lip sync with the musical lyrics blasting out of the playback. I had been given a tape of the numbers us gals were to perform and been asked to learn them. The dance master had drilled us religiously on the steps of the routines. We hadn't actually rehearsed combining the two. This oversight became crystal clear on the morning of the first routine, when we were shown the set in Broken Hill, and shuffled along the narrow dance space at 6:00 A.M. before reporting to hair and make-up.

As the only member of the cast who was not Australian, I had been honoured with my own trailer. Guy and Hugo shared the other.

In solitary splendour and fully made up, I got into drag.

I was beginning to feel my nerves as I put my long fake thumbnail through my fishnet tights. Bellowing out for Tim Chappel, who was Lizzie Gardiner's brilliant collaborator.

He entered, holding an electric razor to his half-shorn chest. "What is it, doll?"

"I'm sorry, Tim. I laddered my tights. Give us another pair, mate."

"Can't."

"Come on. I know it's a small budget, but a pair of tights..."

"It's not that. They're Queenies (made for extra large girls), difficult to find in Sydney. Impossible in Broken Hill." He pulled a face. "Show me."

I indicated the gaping ladder in my tights. He shrugged.

"Forget it," he advised. "It's drag. It's meant to be tacky."

I was alone with my besmirched Queenies and nausea erupting in my gut. I wasn't sure if I could get out of my wagon.

Suddenly there was a "c-o-o-o—e-e-e!" from outside. It sounded like Hugo and Guy. I opened my door and peered out. It was. They were arm in arm, like two girls about to leave a group to go and freshen up. They smiled in unison.

"We thought we'd go in together. They're ready on set."

And so I found myself atop that perilously narrow bar. A harsh ginger wig with detachable pigtails, laddered tights, star-spangled knickers, high heeled dancing shoes, amongst a room full of out of work miners who'd been plied with beer to keep them from leaving.

What Bernadette taught me once and for all was that fear is only a thought.

In closing, I should tell you that just before I got to see the film of *Priscilla* for the very first time—a midnight screening at the Cannes Film Festival—I received a telephone call from the Director of Photography; he was mumbling and seemed to be apologising to me for his lighting job on my character, Bernadette, during the film.

"You didn't do well by me. Why?"

"It was Steph (the director)," he explained. "I told him, 'he's gotta face for camera. Will only need a little front light.' 'No,' he said, 'I don't want him looking good.' I'm really sorry, Terence."

So there I was, dressed to the nines for my first midnight premiere at Cannes. The lights dimmed. The curtain went up; the film began; I was about to view my creation, Bernadette, my androgynous inspiration, a woman trapped inside the body of a man.

I took a luxurious breath in anticipation of the filmic results of my emotional memories, inspired by the wonderful females who had enriched my life: Christie, Shrimpton, Mangano, Princess Diana—any and all of whom I would be happy to be in a female incarnation, but no, up there on the giant silver screen looking back at me was an old tomcat.

Vanity, thy name is Terence.

Yours truly in old school blazer.

CORPSING

I always fancied comedy. I had a few outings in rep. Even on the road with the touring version of *The Long and the Short and the Tall*, I was always listening to the older actors' technique. The timing was the magic, or rather, the magic was concealed in the timing.

I had an outing on Broadway at the wonderful Morosco Theatre back in the Sixties. It was Bill Naughton's *Alfie*. Not the great success it had been in England. Walter Kerr, the *New York Times* all-powerful critic, made sure of that. He was kind to me, yet the abortion scene, the conscience of the piece, while only talked about, apparently offended his Catholic taste.

Alfie staggered on for two months. Believe me, it's no fun playing comedy to a near-empty house. Films were knocking a plenty and I thought, why am I insisting on a medium that isn't working for me?

I didn't appear on the boards for some time after *Alfie*. Funny films didn't come my way either, yet I kept an eye on potentially comical lines or humorous situations.

Nowadays, the Richard Donner *Supermans* are viewed in the high camp style. But when they were released, the world box office impact was so great—Donner's perfect comic book technique and composition within the frame became the benchmark for most comics into movies since—that the subtle humour was overlooked.

It wasn't until *The Hit*, essentially a thriller, but with a touch of black comedy in the mix, that the door to the mansion of comedy was nudged open for me.

* * *

I was in California when I received the call to go and meet with David Zucker. He had co-directed that masterpiece—and one of my dad's favourites—*Airplane.*

A lot of actors don't like to go to meetings on spec (without an offer). Not me. I know that what directors and producers are assessing is the mix, the alchemy of a production. Also, while they are discerning me, I am discerning them.

I thought that David Zucker was a prince, so I was happy when he decided I would be fine for the father in *My Boss's Daughter*. We were also shooting in Vancouver, one of my favourite towns.

The role called for a type of comedic style that I hadn't been party to before; a technique that David and his writers employ that entails a "build up" of potential laughs. The gags and action get thicker and faster as the piece progresses.

I digress for a moment. Ever since I entered show business I had been hearing about the mysterious phenomenon known as *corpsing*. I have no idea why or how it's referred to as this. Only that it happens in performance on stage or film and is described as the unstoppable impulse to laugh. The more it is resisted, the more powerful the urge. There are actors who take it upon themselves to make other actors laugh on stage, but this is not what I am referring to. I had read about corpsing and talked to other performers to whom it happened, but never me; consequently, I had arrived at the conclusion that the phenomenon was an invention or its effect had been exaggerated—something a lot of actors, natural storytellers, are prone to.

However. On one of my early shooting days on the set of *My Boss's Daughter*, I was across a desk from Molly Shannon and Ashton Kutcher. My character was behaving in his typical confrontational manner and accusing the pair of things neither were the least guilty of. The camera was angled on me, and Molly and Ashton were in eye line and giving me their dialogue. On the very first take, my favourite, their reactions were so extreme, so comic that I started to feel the bubbles of laughter deep in my belly. Not wanting to blow a take, and by now known to deliver quickly, I pressed on. Almost immediately, the ripples increased and gathered in intensity. My new partners in crime hung onto and intensified their reactions. I had reached a point where I felt if I didn't give in to it my bladder would involuntarily release itself.

I started to laugh, and with it came all the glorious sensations that accompany the real thing. Watching Tommy Cooper or Richard Pryor. Belly laughs cascaded up to my eyes, which started to tear. Every time it appeared to stop and the camera restarted, the acting across from me gave rise to another unstoppable outburst. Shooting was halted. We had an early lunch. It somehow signalled to me maturity as a performer—an unexpected state of grace in my life as an artist, incomplete without. Since that moment, I have experienced dreams in which a similar happening occurs. Even in sleep, as unstoppable as a sneeze.

The Limey himself with Steven Soderbergh, 1999.

THE LIMEY

One of the charms of having followed a profession for many years is to be able to look back and see where the seeds of future events were sown, albeit seemingly unimportant at the time.

This particular retrospection begins in 1966 with a film titled *Poor Cow*, the story of a woman who continually makes bad choices, falling for a string of criminals, including Dave Fuller, played by myself.

The poor cow in question was actress Carol White and the director, Ken Loach, known for his television successes, was making his debut feature.

* * *

Loach liked to fill his productions with actual characters, which was how Carol and I came to work with John Bindon, a real life tealeaf cast to play a tealeaf (thief)—and Carol's common law husband—in the piece. No problem for yours truly, for whilst Bindon had a reputation as a notorious hard case, he was a complete gentleman on set, comical too, and also notorious for his prodigious appendage—what Marlon Brando would have termed his "noble tool."

In fact, he had a trick that he was fond of performing in public, which involved flashing this massive wherewithal. He would unzip his Strides, whip it out, and clasping the trunk with both hands, twirl the uncut policeman's helmet a few times before safely returning it to his ample trousers and zipping up. I bore witness to this one afternoon while strolling along with him on Kings Road in Chelsea. Walking toward us was the famed reformist peer Lord Longford. Bindon spotted him, nudged me, and in the blink of an eye completed his party trick. So fast and obviously so well rehearsed that I had trouble believing what I had just seen, yet the expression on the great and good's face conveyed the disoriented bewilderment of someone whose gin and tonic had been laced with LSD.

I heard at a later date that Bindon had been a guest on the Caribbean island of Mustique, along with the great fashion photographer Richard Avedon, who persuaded him to air his gyration for fellow vacationer Princess Margaret and her entourage as she came down from her suite to join the group for cocktails. Reputedly, Avedon offered to snap the event. Bindon couldn't resist.

"A blinder," the princess concluded.

"I've seen bigger in Malaya," the lady-in-waiting added.

Later still, Bindon stood trial for the murder of an equally fearsome hard case, Johnny Dark.

In his testimony, John recounted the details of the knifing for the court. The curious judge interjected, "Are you saying, Mr. Bindon, you actually intended to knife Mr. Dark to death?"

"That's right."

"But why on earth, man?"

"Well. He was actually trying to kill me at the time, Your Honor."

He received an in-self-defence verdict.

You can see why it wasn't hard to stay in character with the likes of Bindon on the set.

The other reality check was the fact that Ken Loach improvised the whole film. I am certain he knew precisely what he was doing, but we didn't have a script. He always shot scenes between Carol and me using two cameras simultaneously. This proved to be a once in a lifetime opportunity for me, but it certainly didn't feel like it on the first day. Method acting it wasn't. No "emotional memory" appropriate here.

I had moved on from *the method* of trying to relive emotional moments, tethered as they were in the past, but hadn't actually discovered any modus operandi with a more dynamic slant. Suddenly without preparation or the constraints of learned dialogue, and not knowing what Carol would say or do between "action" and "cut," it became a discipline of "empty head" on "action." Causing me to realize that performance is as spontaneous as speaking is in real life. With the exception of politicians, that is. All that is required is the firm belief that whatever arises from the stillness that underlies all motion would be organically connected to the moment.

* * *

Cut to 1998, Kauai, the Hawaiian island. On holiday in a basic beach hotel whose rooms have no telephones. A message is left at reception to ring Steven Soderbergh at an 818 number in California. I collect a handful of quarters and find my way to a public open-air phone on the beach. Dial the number, and in a minute am connected to the young maestro whose first film, *Sex, Lies and Videotape*, made such a big impression on the business—and me. Would I be interested in playing in a gangster movie entitled *The Limey*? He also mentioned the possibility of using footage from an earlier film I had appeared in, *Poor Cow*, as a kind of back-story.

To be frank, I was lost for words and didn't respond.

"So, what d'you think?" he asked, after a long pause.

"Yes!!"

"Oh, great." He sounded relieved.

It is my turn to ask a question.

"Tell me, Steven. Was there ever any doubt?"

"Oh, sure. It's not many leading men who relish being up there with their thirty years younger selves."

So it began.

* * *

My first and only meeting with Steven, prior to signing, took place in the garden of the Chateau Marmont, in Los Angeles. He told me that when you looked at most people, you could imagine cogs turning in their heads. What he wanted to feel from Wilson, my character, was the presence of a bigger cog behind the others, moving in increments, but powering their motion.

Later, after I'd committed, he rang me. Could I work out what Wilson would wear? He didn't know much of English fashion.

Both of these seeming flecks of direction created a lot of reverberation for me. In fact, they were all the tips I needed.

This seemingly casual request heartened me a great deal. His faith in my ability and his modesty, which always impresses me—one of the most charming features in my opinion, as its nature is to veil itself.

The main thrust of my vitality came with the realization that Soderbergh and co-writer Lem Dobbs—*"Holy cow—Poor Cow—check it out!"* was the memo he'd sent Steven after re-discovering the old film—had constructed the Limey with me in mind; I was determined to plumb the depths and scale the heights to justify their faith. Wilson would speak as my own father had. Wilson's body would tilt forward like the author Ian Fleming, whose bearing struck me as leaning into life. It was a veritable "Life of Riley" to have a character I'd given birth to thirty years previous to tether my present day Limey to, and an absolute luxury to work with a great director at a time in my life when I knew enough to appreciate one. I've heard it said that Soderbergh doesn't consider himself a storyteller, more of a technician fascinated by the intricacies of film itself.

You could have fooled me.

I prepared in the crisp fresh air of Vancouver, memorizing the script until the words became second nature, while hardening up at the wonderful Diane Miller's Pilates studio, using the form of exercise developed by boxer-gymnast Joe Pilates nearly a hundred years ago. Based on muscular control as well as development, Pilates promotes a strong, functional body. There are some things you just can't act. And no amount of *period whistle* (a Sixties suit) would convey a prison tough body if there wasn't one underneath. Or the "big cog" that Soderbergh suggested far behind the eyes.

Steven used his handheld lightweight Arriflex, marking the very first time in a lengthy career that my gal (the camera) and the director were not two. Dialogue preparation combined with the spontaneity of the director resulted in the same impromptu spur-of-the-moment feel achieved on the *Poor Cow* shoot, and also bears witness to Steven's highly developed intuition in not only his sparing use of the old footage, but featuring it in black and white, a stark and melancholic contrast to the Limey of his creation.

* * *

Later, at a film festival in Rotterdam, Holland, I do a Q and A on stage following a screening. A local babe asks me, "Where's the guy who played the young Wilson?"

Appreciating her inferred wantonness and the amazing legs a lot of Dutch girls have, I catch myself feeling nostalgic for my own 25-year-old physique. With a sigh I respond, "He had his 15 minutes of fame. I haven't heard from him lately."

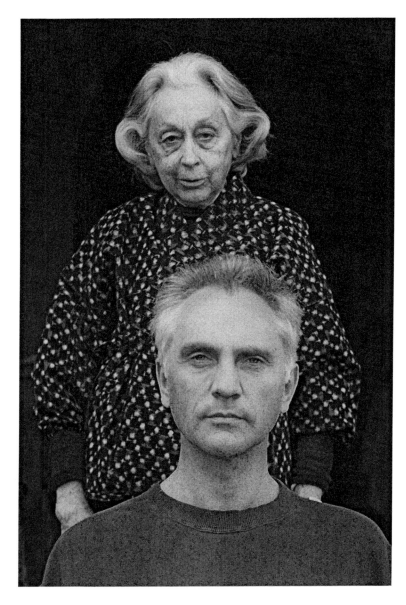

Countess Vanda, my first yoga teacher.

HOME AGAIN

It is Christmas Eve, surely a fitting juncture to finish this manuscript and send it out into the ether for those of you driven to an artistic existence. Fitting also to mention my whereabouts. I had flown in and out of England on the eve of the biggest snowfall in the island's known history. Breaking the journey in New York, I continued scribbling, then westward to spend a few days and nights at the now very famous Chateau Marmont, a terrific retreat for scribblers.

And finally to Ojai, in the high desert, 67 miles and a lifetime away from the hustle of L.A., unexpectedly awash with the greatest deluge of rain since the 1920s.

Of course, no pilgrimage to Ojai is complete without a visit to the venerable pepper tree that Jiddu Krishnamurti sat under that fateful night his life changed irrevocably. The place he referred to as "home," the place I refer to as where he died twice, once to his individuality in 1922; the second to his body, which was 90 years old. Still with 20/20 vision, I believe.

As I sit, the sun has returned and, while there are a few casualty oranges on the ground, the groves are still laden with fruit. A reminder that no branch bears more than it can carry.

What can I tell you that I haven't already told you? Only the essence of what artists finer than myself shared with me.

Engage in what life presents. It has its own reasons. Maybe it isn't what you've hoped for, but hope is like honey. Don't indulge in it. Just eat it when it's on your spoon. Be present and notice when you're not. This being present and knowing when you're present usually has its roots in a heightened state of work. Allow it to flow over into your life—anytime. It is the cog that only appears to turn; yet its radiant presence is the foundation for all the atoms in what we call our body. Aim high; life will support you: It is resonating in your own heart. Have faith in it; be courageous. Disregard your doubtful thoughts. As William Shakespeare wrote, "Our doubts are traitors, and make us lose the good we oft might win, by fearing to attempt." Let doubts pass like clouds in the sky.

The sky is your being, your awareness. Silent, unmoving, yet all sound, all movement manifests from it: the luminous peace at your core. Pay attention to that. Now. Just now. I think that's what my mum was pointing me toward. My real home. Your real home. When the seeking ends the thrill begins. Stand by. On your marks. Action!

END

Richard La Plante, yours truly with Niko, and Michael
Nader with K9 Stamp, East Hampton, 1999.

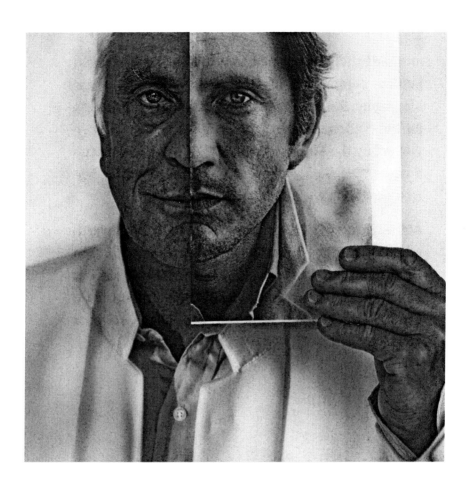

TERENCE STAMP's first title role, in Peter Ustinov's *Billy Budd,* earned him a Golden Globe and an Academy Nomination. He was the *face* of the Sixties, and then, abruptly, the Sixties ended. Out of work and out of fame, he traveled east, to Egypt, India, and Japan before settling in Ibiza, where he helped transform a friend's hectares into an organic food farm.

Stamp's acting career was resurrected in 1977 with the portrayal of General Zod in *Superman I* and *Superman II,* but the true turning point in his life came with the passing of his mother Ethel during the shoot in New York of *Legal Eagles,* compelling him to write his first auto-biography, *Stamp Album,* followed by his meditation on the Sixties, *Double Feature.* Heralded as "a born writer" by the *Sunday Times,* Stamp went on to write a novel, *The Night,* followed by a wheat- and dairy-free cookbook with Elizabeth Buxton.

Although acting keeps him busy, with his award-winning performance in *Priscilla, Queen Of The Desert* and the title role in Steven Soderbergh's *The Limey,* plus recent work beside Jim Carrey, Tom Cruise, and Matt Damon, he has never stopped writing.

CPSIA information can be obtained at www.ICGtesting.com
Printed in the USA
LVOW08s1022011213

363395LV00002B/427/P

GW00759943

CASE FILES

UNSLVED

Future Authors

Edited By Daisy Job

First published in Great Britain in 2021 by:

Young Writers
Remus House
Coltsfoot Drive
Peterborough
PE2 9BF
Telephone: 01733 890066
Website: www.youngwriters.co.uk

Printed and bound in the UK by BookPrintingUK
Website: www.bookprintinguk.com
YB0474B

FOREWORD

As long as there have been people, there has been crime, and as long as there have been people, there have also been stories. Crime fiction has a long history and remains a consistent best-seller to this day. It was for this reason that we decided to delve into the murky underworld of criminals and their misdeeds for our newest writing competition.

We challenged secondary school students to craft a story in just 100 words on the theme of 'Unsolved'. They were encouraged to consider all elements of crime and mystery stories: the crime itself, the victim, the suspect, the investigators, the judge and jury. The result is a variety of styles and narrations, from the smallest misdemeanors to the most heinous of crimes. Will the victims get justice or will the suspects get away with murder? There's only one way to find out!

Here at Young Writers it's our aim to inspire the next generation and instill in them a love of creative writing, and what better way than to see their work in print? The imagination and flair on show in these stories is proof that we might just be achieving that aim! The characters within these pages may have to prove their innocence, but these authors have already proved their skill at writing!

CONTENTS

Josiah Edada	70	Elena Akumu	114
Wilson Bartlett (12)	71	Akzhayaa Nimaleswaran (12)	115
Osasere Edo-Jegede (15)	72	Katie Riley (14)	116
Ayesha Siddika	73	Dawson D'Agostino (13)	117
Olivia Brockway (16)	74	Charlie Beach (12)	118
Mirvat Anshur (13)	75	Chloe Bridle (16)	119
Ellie Lynch (14)	76	Rhys Teesdale (14)	120
Gurveer Singh Matha (12)	77	Tracy Owusu (16)	121
Saffron Ruddock (12)	78	Olivia Beardsmore (15)	122
Lana Force (12)	79	Drew Marshall (13)	123
Kenusha Kalithasan	80	Megan Guest (11)	124
Abigail Smithers (16)	81	Charlotte Sayer (13)	125
Lavanya Basu (14)	82	Alfie Ellson-Guidon (12)	126
Oliver Johns	83	Jessica Barucha (13)	127
Evie Cassie	84	Jess Windram (13)	128
Alfie White (12)	85	Brandon Lewis	129
Millie Purcell (15)	86	Sofia Bennett (13)	130
Maryam Muhammad	87	Ruby Doe-Stovell (13)	131
Irtaza Nayab (12)	88	Emily Stevens (13)	132
Emily MacNaughtan (13)	89	Arthur Jacquemin (13)	133
Jacob Horrill	90	Ellie Buckley	134
Amina Conde	91	James Hall (12)	135
Beth Rayner (13)	92	Isabella Warburton Brown (16)	136
Millie Edwards (11)	93	Lydie Solomon (12)	137
Nnediogo Okezie (12)	94	Joshua Robb (12)	138
Aleena Zaman (15)	95	Rani Jadfa (16)	139
Jessica Martin (15)	96	Koray Rogers (13)	140
Hana Kawal (17)	97	Jack Archer	141
Gracie Brindley (12)	98	Dean Wilson (14)	142
Kieran Davis (16)	99	Joshua Jogy	143
Ruby Barry (15)	100	Coral Joseph	144
Abi Fewings (11)	102	Rhianna Baker	145
Andreia Vasilean (12)	103	Mia Wright (12)	146
Nathan Hilton (13)	104	Sofia Terry (14)	147
Maisie Shea (15)	105	Ebony Elliot (12)	148
Isabella Trewhella (15)	106	Charlie Godfrey (12)	149
Demi-Jo Smithers (12)	107	Lucas Elwall (16)	150
Riya Kale	108	Joe Silverlock (16)	151
Amelia Atkin (11)	109	Maysaa El Aoussi Hamdoun (11)	152
Ruby Blackbeard (13)	110	Dexter Kitto (14)	153
Mahiya Mohan (12)	111	Thalia Andrew	154
Maria Sibi	112	Finlay Borrett (12)	155
Iyioluwa Olagbegi	113	Osian Roberts	156

THE STORIES

LIES ARE LEGAL

"Committing a murder is much easier than planning one," sniggered Leroy Hargraves, being interrogated for the cold-blooded murder of Mona Tillery: the fourth corpse this week. "Please state your reasoning," replied Rebecca Porter, who was utterly confused by this man's peculiarly calm expression.
"Because... you're born to die. Makes my job easier."
What puzzled Rebecca the most was that he appeared unperturbed that an innocent body had been found mutilated and he was the main suspect. The police obtained no hard evidence, except Leroy's report which was conveniently persuasive. But... maybe too persuasive to convince Rebecca that it was unrehearsed...

Maya Bayman (12)

GAME OF MURDER

"It was me."
She froze. The door creaked open, and she hid herself. The last person she ever expected walked through.
Herself.
Impossibly identical, right down to each freckle.
The police were waiting when she raced home.
"It wasn't me!" Cybele screamed.
Detective Martinez thrust a photograph at her. "Looks like you."
Cybele stared down at herself, hunched over the dead body, caked in blood. Martinez's hands began to tighten around something.
Then the world exploded. The police were dead. Spluttering, Cybele looked up to see her doppelganger pulling off the mask.
"You're the real victim, Cybele. Time to die."

Manqi Wang

STEALTHY KILLER

Darkness had eventually fallen, with it the dampening of my once assured spirit. I sat for hours, contemplating them, but who possessed a stealthy killer within? The man with vengeance clouding his sight? The ragged woman in ownership of three daggers? The young man sprawled carelessly across the couch, smiling cruelly at my disillusion? Although troubled, none had taken life tonight. I had failed.

"My daughter, detective, who shot her? Who?" Her cry of despair echoed through the walls, cutting through me like a knife.

Just.

"Ma'am." Cautiously I approached her. "We never revealed she was shot."

Her face fell.

Yusan Ghebremeskel (16)

TOGETHER FOREVER

Leukaemia. That was what she had, and it was taking her away from me.

"I'm sorry."

"I know, dear," she whispered, gazing up at me, her eyes calm, tinged with a subtle sadness.

"But-"

She reached out and gently rested her arm on my back.

"Heather..."

"I love you, Tom."

We gave each other a final hug.

"Sweetheart?"

"Yes?"

"Even death won't separate us, right?"

She hugged tighter. The pain of losing her was like acid burning through my chest.

"Of course," I whispered, heartbroken.

Then I felt something enter my back.

"I know. You're coming too," she exhaled.

Saahil Patel (13)

SUGAR LUMPS

She's just like you.
Familiar childish giggles permeated the silence. I couldn't help but stare. Stare - all I seem to ever do. Her face was lifted to the sky as she spun around, arms raised, and her baby-blue dress floating. A tea party was going on, stuffed animals were strewn across the lawn.
I shifted.
She turned towards where I was hunched, taking tiny steps towards me.
"Hello?"
I shifted again, the bush shaking. She took three small steps back, eyes widening...
I lunged.
Everything was set up, plastic teacups filled with sugar lumps.
A distraught mother screamed: "Meredith!"

Madison Looker (17)

THE VOICE

The three dice feel like cold teeth in Ela's hand. She rolls each one separately, as Alice instructed. Mumbling, the old fortune-teller stares at their placement inside the chalk circle.

Candles flicker on the stone mantle. Ela shifts, sweat dampening her armpits.

"Interesting," Alice mutters.

Suddenly, a sound like beating wings erupts from the fireplace. The candles extinguish and darkness swallows the room.

"Ela!" a familiar voice exclaims as it channels through the fortune-teller's throat...

Ela starts to cry. Somewhere down the hall, a window breaks.

"Run!" her mother screams. "They've found you!"

Rainelle Francis-Manu

POTTERS

This intruder said nothing, claiming with a flap of papers this bone china factory had been using human remains in their wares. The now unattended barrels clunked unhealthily in the distance, the mass of overalls drawing closer. Machines were switched off for lunch, the rattle of crockery sighing eventually. The workers entertained themselves in accusations, before turning their attention to an unseen suspect.

"Where were you Tuesday night?"

Until now I hadn't realised I was anything more than a narrator of some low-budget crime mystery, but here I was, able to open my mouth. "I've only existed since chapter one."

Ellie Gilbert (16)

THE CURE

Years of pain, loss, funerals marking victims of an incurable disease. Cancer! The deadliest plague of them all. Scientists discovering research. No cure - nothing. Only to discover the same news as yesterday. Millions more died. They did not win the quest to succeed. Unbeatable. Monstrous.
In 2000, this changed. "I found it," cried a scientist. The database was saved and tested to make sure the drug was safe. Licensed. Agreed to go ahead.
"Save many," cried the ministers.
The next day the database got hacked. Stolen. Erased from all existence. Ten years of research. Millions of pounds. Gone. Why?

Katie Peters (12)

TRIGGER WARNING...

I walked around the corner. Screams echoed through the tight corridor. Blood splashed the grey-brick walls. The scene was grotesque. I couldn't help but smile at the gothic scene I was creating. I started to laugh psychotically, staring helplessly at the tears forming in her eyes.

"You're a psychopath!" she whimpered.

"And you fell in love with me... Who's worse?" I retaliated.

"You are. You always were a monster and I didn't love you... I pitied you!" she sighed sadly.

"Then finish the job Angelique, but know I love you."

Angelique then plunged the dagger further into my chest.

Ellie Laggan (13)

THE DUO

Pair of murmurs speak as they quarrel to dominate my brain.

The detective glances over towards me, unsatisfied with my accused behaviour.

Impatiently, I wait for the judge to determine a verdict.

If it wasn't you, why're you here? You're unpredictable, you're full of malicious motives, you monster! Go on... tell them, you're responsible! You're faultless, I promise. You were dead asleep the night of the felony. The crime was across the street. The evidence is unreliable. The commotion wasn't you!

Clocks tick, a pin drops, eyes roll. My cold feet nervously tap the ground. It is just too late.

Rebecca Bailey (16)

THE HEMLOCK PLANTS ON HEMLOCK AVENUE

He looked around the library, the volumes of books piled around him. He'd been there every night for the last week. Detective Jakes had been commissioned for the Elijah Vaughan murder and despite his expertise, he just couldn't solve it. He had the motive and suspect, but what had been used to kill him?

In frustration, the detective turned to the paragraph he had been reading: '...water hemlock is infused with cicutoxin, and rapidly generates fatal symptoms'. Glancing at the illustration, he groaned. How had he missed that? He could remember seeing those growing outside Amia Grain's house. "Gotcha!"

Olivia Chantler (17)

THE DOGS HUNT AT NIGHT

"Right, everyone, sit around the table in silence, please..."
Calmly spoken, he starts to read. "The Dogs hunt at night,
scavenging for their next meal. Slowly crawling and stalking
their next victim. Only attacking when the alarm is pulled. A
growl ends the silence and the chase begins, jumping over
obstacles and pointing after the poor thing targeted.
Eventually, the chase is over and there's silence and the
slight reflection of the gruesome beasts' actions."
The man pauses and takes a deep breath... "This was the
statement given by a murderer in London gang known as
The Devil-Dogs."

Alex Pashov (13)

MURDER MYSTERY

The darkness crept in. Dullness and perplexity gathered around him. They watched him as he wondered, *who would commit this horrible crime?* Disorientation hurled around him like a shark swarming its prey. Nothing felt right. John knew his fellow companions wouldn't have the will to accomplish a dreadful sin like this. Or would they? He decided to investigate.

It hit the stroke of midnight when John crept beside his companion, Jerome. John asked his relative if he knew who could have killed his beloved wife.

Jerome replied, "Maybe I do."

John slowly turned his head and his life was over.

Musa Waleed Meer

THE ART OF LIES

I kneeled towards the blood splattered almost artistically against the floor. I had swirled my brush in the paint and created this organised mess.

"There's nothing here."

My Irish lilt echoed, droning in my head as I heard her cries. They pierced me. They taunted me. They consumed me. The eyes in the painting had been gouged out.

Darkness cloaked my mind until the eyes from the painting were her serpentine ones. Her fingers snaked around my throat. Choking.

The picture. The trap door I'd escaped from.

"Detective Brown." The voice called for me.

"The case has been closed."

Ashima Pujary (13)

THE WANDERING EYE

I immediately snap out of my daze as a refulgent overhead lamp blinds my swollen eyes. My pupils adjust to the blaring light. I vaguely see them circling around me; they're like wolves. Their questions are continuous and repetitive, forming a wave of miscellaneous accusations. I notice one of the men picking the skin around his fingernail. I watch intently until it rips off and a small stream of blood trickles down his hand. Suddenly a dark demonic figure emerges from the corner of the interrogation room.

"Answer the goddamn questions!" the detective bellows.
"We know you killed Mary Dyke."

Tamilore Fapohunda (15)

SILENCE

The silence was loud. The icy feel of her sniper pierced through her hands. She looked outside the window; as if the sky were a faucet, slowly draining the vibrant colours into a vacuum of nothingness, night was approaching rapidly. People gathered, forming rivers of clothing.
She bit her lip as she found the sharp glare overlooking the crowd. The President stepped onto the platform and all heads turned towards him, automatically.
"We will rise above!" the dictator bellowed, his voice filling the arena.
Just as the crowd cheered, a sharp gunshot was heard and she breathed with relief.
Freedom?

Bianca Nedelcu (14)

A JUDGE'S DISHONOUR

The courtroom was chilly but I was sweating. I couldn't look at the defendant, though nobody would suspect anything. They call me 'Your Honour'. *Honour.* That word kills me. The defendant knows I did it though... But how did he get that pistol in his pocket? I thought about what would make a better headline:

'Innocent defendant kills judge' or 'Guilty judge kills defendant'.

My conclusion: BANG.

They were shocked, I think, those little people down below. Perhaps you think I feel guilty. Well, hold on to that cheap notepad of yours, because I've still got the gun.

Faith Carter (13)

TIME

We all only have a little time left. Especially these people.
One day there was a weather forecast so strange no one
believed it. "The moon's going t-" screamed the
weatherman.
Alex, Joe and Bill listened to him. The forecast cut. They
sighed and went outside. Everything was grey and didn't
feel right. They looked up and the moon was forming a face.
"The moon's smiling," said Alex.
"Yeah, that's obvious Alex," replied Bill with a sharp tone in
his voice.
The moon started to close in and that was the last moment
on Earth. Terrifyingly slow death.

Bear Briggs (12)

THE NOTE

Edward Langingham, the world-renowned writer, sat in the empty diner with unwavering focus. Spectacles perched precariously on his crooked nose as his imagination bubbled bizarrely as clouds in his coffee. Suddenly, the door swung open, revealing a young man with chestnut hair and a briefcase. Immediately, he paced towards Langingham's table and dropped a napkin in his lap. Riddled with confusion, he flipped it to reveal a blood-curdling message. 'Run now'.

Edward swung his head from each side looking for him, yet all that was left was a waiter with a smile that was far too pulled in the corners...

Arisha Dutta (12)

THE CONFUSION

She was certainly dead yesterday. Or so I was told. Yet here she is now, buying a drink and talking to her friend. Laughing, and looking very much alive. I stare, slack-mouthed. Politely, she smiles and strolls over, heels clicking across the tiles.

"How are you?"

"Good." She raises her glass to her crimson lips; her eyes slice through me like knives.

I notice on her finger a new ring glittering idly in the lamplight.

"I don't suppose you've seen Lucy, recently?" she asks after a pause.

I look at her closely before declining all knowledge of her sister's whereabouts.

India Tindley

MURDER, MYSTERY AND CRIME

"Murder, mystery, crime..." the words echoed through New York's bustling streets.

Agent Lily was determined to solve the case as she came to a dark, narrow street. Ahead, she could see a hooded figure. The silence was deadly; she could hear her breathing so clearly.

Lily walked towards the figure. She stood before the hooded figure, hesitantly. As she pulled her gun from her pocket, she heard a familiar dry laugh. "You," she whispered. Hands shaking, she put the gun to his heart. Alas, it was empty. Her fate was sealed.

After all, tonight there was murder, mystery and crime.

Saalihah Patel (12)

LIQUIDATION

Henry crept down a narrow, unilluminated alleyway encumbered with thick fog consuming his vision at midnight. At the opposing side was a towering, stocky man, his face hidden, clad in black, taunting him with a trenchant knife in his enfolded leather-gloved hand.

Unexpectedly, the black-hooded man pounded heavily toward Henry, forcefully plunging the knife into his back, penetrating his reverberating heart which poured warm scarlet liquid.

Shakily, Henry lifted his hand to feel the warm sticky liquid ooze and trickle down his body. His vision darkened. His breath slowed. He lay there still.

The world went black.

Charlotte Weaver (14)

MURDER AT THE MOVIES

''What happened?'' the detective will yell.

Murder at the movies. No suspect. No witness. No motive. Eat that up, Agatha Christie.

In one hour, my husband's limp, lifeless, lonely body will be discovered at his daughter's feature directorial debut. Girl power.

They'll question me. I didn't do it. Not really.

My husband killed me first. I'd never hire someone to kill my cheating husband. I would call that unnecessary. With the betrayal of my husband came the death of my morals. And what are you without your morals? Can you exist?

Well, if I don't exist. Why should he?

Charlotte Cash (16)

THE REAL PERPETRATOR

Tabitha's teeth were jittering.

She wheeled her way to the front, not without running over a few feet first!

Tabitha began to read aloud.

The class sat wide-eyed, never having concentrated like this before!

The story of Toby was told, a wheelchair-using, doll-complexioned young boy who had committed such a crime to make the devil cry.

The goody-two-shoes of the class shakily raised his hand.

"How would a boy with just two wheels be able to pull this off?"

Tabitha had a terrifying grin plastered over her face.

Thank God the real perpetrator wasn't revealed.

Maia Williams (13)

TILLY AND ELIZA

The two girls looked down at the cold, lifeless body before them. A marking the colour of figs bloomed on his left cheek - horrifying against the milk-white skin.

Eliza bent down and examined it closely. She could see distinct hexagonal markings from the sole of a shoe in the slowly darkening bruise. "God, he's been kicked to death," she said.

Tilly shuffled backwards, and slowly and subtly lowered her bag over her feet.

"Hey, don't you have some trainers like that, Tills?" Eliza asked quietly.

Thirty minutes later, one girl looked down at the two cold, lifeless bodies before her.

Martha Purdy (11)

THE MISSING PLANE

All was silent as Flight 6489 glided through the skies heading east. The passengers noted nothing, sleeping soundly. It was only till the warning system went off, warning the passengers the plane was going off course, something was wrong. The passengers' backs prickled with fear and their hearts stood still. The level of their apprehension was as deep as the Pacific.

Then, screaming started. The plane was dropping from 30,000ft. The control tower was frantic. The plane had disappeared from radar. All was lost as the plane plummeted towards death.

Five minutes of chaos on the plane, then death.

Hammaad Rashid

TARGET NUMBER TWELVE

Misfortune diffused, outlining the scene of undeniable doom; yet the victim lay oblivious, laundered in an encrusting of their own blood.

Cooling restraint held up a silent, still smile, like the burden of existence was shattered on a bond of appreciation. Eyes rippling like stars, she expired with her last breath resembling tranquillity.

Trust was a dramatised sense of hushed humanity nowadays. Now the corpse of an innocent somebody was recycled as a hurdle, as the nobody bearing her unqualified, concluded moments stalked the steps of a free man into her kitchen, surely to tick target twelve off the list.

Hope Ashby (14)

DER MENSCH VERSUCHTE ES!

I pressed play.

They were in a room. Hospital-like. Soaked with pain and death. A girl, silky white hair, tatty nightgown. Cold, moreover petrified. The doctor, Spinner. Nutcase. You can always tell from the aura they give off.

He was injecting her with what my deductive brain could process as dimethyltrienolone.

Silence. Like the universe paused to see what unfolded next.

A cacophonous din. Purple, swelling lungs. Creamy white foam. Blue eyes gone grey.

Spinner groaned down his radio, "Test erfolglos."

Placing a sheet over her he began mammocking her.

Frantically I called it in. Cold case over.

Dylan Gallery (14)

PIED PIPER

A new day, the same case. It'd been running for seven months, the case of the missing children. The culprit was named the 'pied piper', taking children without leaving a trace.

"Welcome, sir." The detective entered the same room and stared at the red string connecting pictures to towns to notes. He was well known and respected, worked hard every day and this day was no exception.

Nightfall approached and the detective left, returning to his home, hanging up his coat, placing his keys on the counter before heading to his basement, the muffled cries of children echoing. He smiled.

Noor-Ul-Ain Bhatti (17)

THE GUIDE TO MURDER

Getting away with murder is never easy. It requires months, even years, of vigorous planning, powerful contacts and lots of dedication. I've learned that the incentive for murder usually stems from robbery, jealousy or vengeance; mine is the latter.

What makes my plan ingenious is my inconspicuous motive. I was wronged by this person so long ago that my incentive will be overlooked - deemed irrelevant. And even if I get interrogated, my spotless record and ability to lie under pressure will guarantee that I am proclaimed innocent. It's the perfect plan, which tomorrow I shall put to the test.

Nicole Kravtsov

THE THIN LINE BETWEEN BLACK AND WHITE

While preparing to be a mother, you don't realise the loyalty you hold for your child is unshatterable. Even if they fight, become rage-filled, or in my case convicted for manslaughter, the bond is undeniable even while it's still hanging by a thread. Cycles of disbelief, anger, then guilt play. You wonder what actions caused them to stray so far from morality.

As my career prospered, my relationships broke down. I hadn't seen my son for years but when he turned up on my doorstep, bloodstained, discombobulated, fearful, loyalty stayed.

I am stuck between pearly right and dark wrong.

Sabiha Halim (15)

THE MIDNIGHT MAFIA

Every male in the Mafia thinks females cannot be a leader. I'm living proof to show them otherwise. My gang and I are the strongest in Italy, despite the whole Mafia not knowing I'm a female. I inherited my gang from my father, who I look up to.

Now back to reality, we're in the middle of a big shipment. Normally leaders don't go to shipments but someone has been messing with *my* shipment. "Alright, guys, you know the plan. Everyone ready?"

"Yeah."

As I walk around the side of the container, I see my worst enemy. Alexander flipping Scorpio.

Eira Brown

UNSOLVABLE

The suspect was gone! Curious. Seeking. Interested. Finding clues. It was dangerous, with a criminal, who committed a threatening crime, gone within seconds. Solving this difficult and critical situation was no longer straightforward. There was no suspect, no fingerprints, no DNA.

What to do? I don't really know. This had just become a deep, significantly urgent atrocity to all victims and citizens from an obvious position! They are all in a very perilous, unsafe crisis. What do we all do when we don't have anything like suspects or DNA or no witnesses in this case? Everyone for protection!

Tegan Guest (12)

WHAT'S GOING ON?

Darkness. An empty room. Just me alone. *What happened last night?* I asked myself, not knowing where I was or what time it was.

"Check your phone," a small voice called out.

I did. It was 4:27am.

"Check your location," the same voice whispered.

I did. According to Google Maps, I was at home. This was not my house.

"Look out the window."

I did. I wish I hadn't. A man stared through the broken glass. A gun.

"Run!"

A bang. He didn't get me. Another man looked into my eyes. A gun. A bang. This time, he got me...

Esme Joseph

QUICKER THAN BEFORE

75 miles per hour. Although a minuscule detail, flashing lights were visible in the mirror.

Staring ahead, only an endless expanse of terrain lay before us. Glancing back at the mirror, blurry forms edged into focus. We were coming to a halt.

"What are you doing?!"

"...There's no point playing a losing game."

Terror and shock overtook me. Sirens became more and more audible. A gun was placed atop my forehead. Yet worst of all, his raging glare as he switched on a walkie-talkie.

"We've captured the suspect. Proceed to unload the trunk."

I believed I had an alibi.

Alicja Bednarczuk (15)

ON THE RUN

Rushing away, she turned to hide behind a corner to reload her gun. She was aware they were behind her but still she stayed calm. As soon as she heard them coming, she spun around the corner and fired shots. Watching them drop dead to the floor made her realise how easy it actually was. "Hmmm."

As she reached into the dead man's pocket, she found a necklace and a voice suddenly called out to her from behind. "Aurora."

She prepared her stance, ready to shoot as she turned around slowly. "Oh great," she said sarcastically, "it's you!"

Holly Andrews (13)

OMIT

They asked me: Who? When? Why?
I don't remember.
They searched around.
A knife, a paper in a victim's hand:
"... it's your fault," he read.
I've heard it before; why?
The case was closed; no clues were found.
I went home. There were mobile messages: 'I didn't mean it',
'Liar'.
I tried to remember what it was about; my brain refused.
A newspaper was dropped in the corner: 'Killed by her
friend'. Under it a picture of a woman, a familiar one.
Memories flashed in my head.
I fell, screamed and cried. "Murderer, I'm the murderer."

Habiba Rabiey (14)

GARDEN SHED

Siena's eyes jerked wide open as the fetid smell of decay and rotting wood crawled up her nostrils. Cold stone met her palms as she tried to sit up when a blinding pain tore through her right arm. Her head bashed back onto the ground as the pain throbbed on, and her groans rang in her ears.

A drop of water splashed onto her pale cheek. Shabby, moss-strewn planks of a garden shed towered above her.

Just then, faint sirens began to wail.

A voice sliced through the silence. "Sweet Siena, don't scream. I'll get caught."

'Teenager's disappearance baffles police'.

Yinuo Shi

UNNOTICED

She went unnoticed until then.

As the amber, damp leaves squelched under my boots I made my way through the desolate forest, mind racing to understand why it was done. She was a normal girl, not many friends to the department's knowledge, lived on a decent street, nothing out of the ordinary. I clenched my police cap as forest twigs reaching out threatened to whip it off.

"Why? Why? Why?" I screamed to nobody in particular.

But what chilled me to the bone wasn't that I didn't know, but rather that I received an answer... "Eh, just felt like it."

Roshni Garg (13)

THE DOWNFALL

Failure. It was bouncing, rocketing around inside my skull with a furious passion and possession. Three years of work for nothing. I had failed, failed to stop the attack, failed to stop the terrorists and was looking at the consequences. The Pentagon lay in front of me, crumbling and without the presence of glory and power that it had portrayed before. Blood stained the ground. Its owners were left with damaged bodies and their moans that pierced through the air.

"Sir...? Sir! What do we do now?"

It was the start of the downfall, and nobody could stop it now.

Casper Pretorius (14)

GODFATHER DEATH

They say dying is peaceful. But dying is explosive. Death courses through their veins; an uncanny black adrenaline shearing their souls away. All mutilating possibilities of life lead to one finality: I swing my scythe and water the poppies.

Many futilely obsess over building a machine to halt the pendulum in their souls, but it is no use trying to solve it, nor solve me. Pain is the truth. The truth that the bloody, ethereal seconds are trickling through their fingers, smothering the carpet with sin. Physical death is mundane. Anguishing souls are sublime.

My alias? Godfather Death.

Rebekah Bolton

IN THE DEAD OF NIGHT...

"What did you see that night?" were the final words spoken before I revealed the truth of what happened on September 9th 1990...

Scream!

Amongst the heart of darkness that clouded the sky; I vacated the comfort from my car to face the open country road...

I ignited my torch to confront the deep, dark darkness.

Scream!

My feet broke into a scamper...

But, but then, I looked down and I saw the most shockingly evil and vile sight. An exemplarily crafted, articulately hidden and executed crime.

A scar burned through my brain. A scar burned on September 9th 1990...

Thomas Mossman

IT WAS YOU

"999, what's your emergency?" And the case opened.

The sirens screamed. The luminous blue lights beamed. My heart raced as we sped off to the crime scene.

Her fingertips were stained a deep, crimson red - the red of her own blood. Blood splatters crawled down the walls.

There lay the lifeless, crippled body of Stephanie Parker. Her skin was pale and her eyes shone like marbles.

The evidence bags lay scattered on the table, each making no more sense than the next. Then it hit me. It could not be simpler.

"It was you. Wasn't it? You murdered Stephanie Parker..."

Daisy Blacklock (12)

THE BANG

Bang! What was that I heard when I woke up? *Bang!* There it was again, but louder this time; I sat up in bed wondering what it was. Fireworks? Firecrackers? No, it couldn't have been... Was it... a gun?

I tried to escape the building but I couldn't. *Bang,* again but it sounded next door. I started panicking then hid all my stuff and entered the wardrobe to make the apartment seem empty.

Then the door opened. "Ugh, this one's empty. Come on, let's go," a gruff, deep voice said.

So I walked out, but I saw him. *Bang!*

Jake Herron (11)

A NIGHTMARE TOO REAL

His skin, scarred by the flames of death. He was alone. Abandoned. Unwanted. No word could be said that didn't mean he was by himself. The other orphans made it out safely, but he was trapped inside the falling prison.

"Max?" a girl said, walking through the fire. Before he could step away, his body was lifeless on the ground!

"Max, I found you!" she shouted. "What's that on your arm?"

He sat up, finding himself on the grass at a playground. He looked down to see giant burns on him.

"Mom is calling us, we got to go!"

"Mom?"

Megan Ceesay

TRAPPED

Hello? Hello? The sound of the roaring thunderstorm awoke his consciousness. Mum? Her crying voice hit his heart with excruciating pain. He could hear their melancholy voices yet they couldn't hear him. He gave a piercing scream, hoping somebody would hear him. The sudden realisation hit him like a dodgeball. He was trapped... Tears ran down his shocked soul as his body lay motionless and still. *You have to wake up.* Petrified, he looked around trying to track the silent voice which sounded like his own. *Fight it, you have to fight it*. He realised he was in a coma.

Abbey Bone

THE ACCOMPLICE

"I told you! I'm not doing anything!" I spat at the gruff, surly figure that stood before me, sounding a lot more confident than I felt. My whole body shook at the sight of him. Why couldn't he just leave me? It's not like the day wasn't haunting me already.

"He knows, Turner."

I collapsed on the floor, making no attempt to stifle my sobs.

"Do it."

The words were enough. I understood. I said nothing.

He kicked me, his shoes digging in.

I yelped and looked up at him. I nodded weakly. I was to kill a man. Again.

Jorja Turner

IN THE SHADOWS

It was the thrill.

The thrill of running, escaping and the adrenaline rushing through her veins that made her a full-time fugitive criminal and reached her to the top of the country's wanted list. She'd already vanished when the police arrived. The body had been disposed of in an alley with a note on top: 'Streak's getting longer! <3' with a fake fingerprint to set the police on a fruitless goose chase.

No one knew her identity; they could only guess her height and age. But little did they know, that the girl was, in fact, the chief constable's daughter...

Arkar May Htet (13)

THE EXPERT

This wasn't my idea. I thought we were handling the case perfectly fine on our own. The government disagreed. But if they thought this was better, they were sorely mistaken. Sending in an 'expert' was what they said. What we got was a mercenary. Was this some kind of joke? These people didn't care about justice, only money.

I glared at the so-called expert as he swaggered in, an easy, sly smile on his face. He looked like one of the 'cool guys' from the playground.

"Welcome to Pembrooke Police Department," I sassed. He grinned and nodded.

Madeline Rose Willmott (16)

DOUBLE 'KILLINGS'

The Phi twins. The meaning means ghost in some countries.
Both killed on Halloween night in two separate locations,
the only night they finally contacted each other in thirteen
years.

This case was twenty years ago but no crucial evidence had
turned up despite the killings having plenty of evidence at
the crime scene. It was recently reopened by a detective
who was determined to avenge the two girls. Although...
whenever the detective tried asking around, no one seemed
to even hear of the event. Maybe their names weren't just a
coincidence?

What do you think, sister?

Quinn Gardiner (14)

THE BRISTOL KILLER

Once lived this mysterious killer who used to go around town and murder innocent people on the streets of Bristol. No one knew the name of the killer. This person had killed four people on the street and taken them to an eerie, old, abandoned warehouse.

Soon, the victims' families had reported them as missing which led to the police having to search for them. Little did they know that the missing were dead.

Shortly, they discovered the bodies. There were three suspects who had to go to court. They pleaded innocent, which left the killer roaming around Bristol freely.

Tia Chana (12)

HARLEM'S HOOLIGANS

The suspect was gone; his brother was gone; the evidence was gone. He had nothing to prove his brother's death. His life was nothing apart from a wreck at this point, but the consistent voice in his head told him to carry on. Constant hard-working days passed as he attempted to avenge his brother, and finally... he had incriminating links to his brother's death, to multiple shootings. Within seconds he was out the door, hate-driven to find the hooligans responsible. From that hectic late-night store, Marquillio successfully put to sleep one of the biggest gangs in Harlem.

Oakley Astin Vine (16)

THE WHISPERER

A 13-year-old girl, Evelyn, went missing a week ago and no one knows why or how. Evelyn's father, Jacob, hires a detective.

The detective finds himself in a dark tunnel leading to who knows where. He finds a cell room that looks like it has been closed for a while. Something just doesn't add up.

He hears something behind him. He thinks it's Evelyn, but it is actually a guy holding a knife.

The detective wakes up on the floor, blood on his hands and before he completely closes his eyes, he hears a whisper saying, "The whisperer always watches."

Emily Marshall (11)

WRONGED BY JUSTICE

"You are sentenced to life in prison, on the charge of murder!"

I kept silent. It wasn't my fault, but they didn't believe me. No one did.

We were alone on the rooftop, eating. She took a bite of her sandwich, mayonnaise smearing across her mouth.

"How do you eat that stuff?" Tenderly, I wiped her soft lips with my sleeve.

She climbed atop the bench. "It's not my fault you hate it." She stepped back. I saw it too late.

Her head hit the ground. My hands cradling her head stained crimson. I couldn't save the one I loved.

Thea Le Neveu (12)

MYSTERIES OF LAKE HADES

Lake Hades. A village near the coast that's been described as a peaceful place where people can enjoy themselves and live an easy life hidden from the dangers of the outside world.

I disagree. I know what evil is here as I have seen it, faced it and banished it. But she's back.

"Three fishermen have taken their own lives this past week. Witnesses have heard what is believed to be a woman's voice singing." That was our radio station sharing the news with the village.

To them it's a mere coincidence, but to me it's the work of sirens...

Hannah Witter (13)

CONFINED FEELINGS

Everybody seems to have one attribute that makes them unique. It may be excessive knowledge on a certain topic, excelling at physical activities. Whatever it may be, no one has my talent. My talent? I can't have a talent. Whatever I come across I never have any interest in it; it's almost as if something is missing, trapped... Someone is holding a multi-million-pound lottery? Not interested. Someone proposed to me. Sorry not now. Trying to sue me? Okay, take my money. Great talent ain't it? It's always winter for me (although if it was, I wouldn't feel it).

Ronith Velegar (13)

MYSTERY MURDERER

I have found a clue. Blood on the floor. What happened here? A poor woman lying in a pool of her own blood. Nine stab marks. What kind of person would commit such a crime?

This dimly lit alleyway is just an invitation for trouble. Victim after victim, these violent cases still remain unsolved - all thirty-two that have taken place here in this death trap. Will this case join them? The killer, still roaming around free, waiting for their next unsuspected victim, never to be caught.

I feel defeated. Another case left unsolved. Another brutal murder waiting to happen.

Abbie Kingman

UNSOLVED CRIME

Burgundy blood gushed out of the pale human that lay beside her. This case was the one reason she couldn't sleep. All her fears, all her dilemmas, obliterated. She was convinced that some type of monstrosity was the slayer of these poor souls.

Citizens at home had the right to be afraid. No evidence proved these killings were by a human. No evidence corroborated that it was an animal. Due to the number of humans massacred, police couldn't close this investigation, because of the importance, yet there were no leads to help them solve it. It was an unsolved crime.

Laila Parchment (11)

THE DEAD CAN'T TALK, I KNOW DIFFERENT

Wrong place, wrong time. I found my parents on a freezing Sunday night. Still. Lifeless. So painful. Pete the Law stepped up to defend me. He was quick-witted, knew the law and was confident.

I had poisoned my parents. I was the sole inheritor. Evidence pointed at me. But how? I was handcuffed.

The dead can talk. I found my head in my Mum's diaries... craving a moment of her wisdom. There in black and white. 'I loved Peru - drinking and sightseeing. Pete had a perverse interest in Amazonian poison'. The word rang in my head. Deafening. Painful. Liberating?

Alexandra Cummings

THE LIFE THIEF

"What am I going to do? How am I going to return back?" I
questioned myself...

Two weeks earlier, I heard a shocking announcement by the
WHO that the Coronavirus was a pandemic.

"You should cancel your flight," my mother yelled.

"It's safe there, do not worry," I argued.

Next day, I went with my friend abroad. Suddenly the
number of COVID-19 cases increased and dead bodies were
everywhere as if I were in a horror film and all the flights
were cancelled! I wish I listened to her. Now I'm trapped
with nowhere to go...

Faten Elnasharty (13)

NOTHING

"I stood staring at the house. I could hear muffled screaming coming from inside. Then, suddenly, someone was pushed against the house's window. Their mouth was open and screaming came from it. They were soon pulled away from the window, but there was a handprint stain on the glass. Blood. I wanted to run away, get help. But I couldn't move. The house's door swung open and a man with blood on their hands walked up to me and whispered in my ear, 'You saw nothing'," Miss Jones told the police officer, shuddering.
The police officer smiled.

Mithuna Maheswaran

FREEDOM

London in 2115 is imprisoned by fear.

Since the warlock Zoar took power, nobody can leave town. With his magic, Zoar has turned the city's statues into his henchmen. Happiness and joy are not allowed; all citizens, prisoners of his crime.

Then a sudden encounter changes a young boy's life forever. A mysterious foreigner with a map and a mission to accomplish... but the boy is crucial to the mission. Harry will have to fight unimaginable creatures and travel in parallel worlds to defeat Zoar and fight for justice.

He is very young - will he be up to the challenge?

Enrico Thovez

THE BROKEN SILENCE

It started on a cold bitter night when the light was cloaked with darkness. A scream of agony. The floor was stained with dark fresh blood. Then, silence.

Soon after sirens shattered the tranquillity. Officers and detectives cautiously approached the scene. The main detective was Joe. He put on a brave face although on the inside he was packed with fear. He was standing in front of a corpse covered in an ocean of blood.

The detectives did a thorough search but found no clues. Everyone left apart from Joe.

Bang! The smell of blood filled the air...

Isaam Ahmed

MANGLED CHEST

Ten murders in ten weeks, all committed with a sharp blade, and still nobody has a clue who the killer could be. Professor Eliza Smith is an adventurous detective with a fondness for solving crimes. She doesn't know it yet but she is the only one who can stop the killer.

So when her best friend, Oscar Williams, is kidnapped, Smith finds herself thrown into the centre of the investigation. Her only clue is a giant book.

She enlists the help of an ambitious painter called Michael Hudson. Can Hudson help Smith find the answers before the killer strikes again?

Helena Lucena Hurla (11)

THE GLITCH

It all started with a break-in. I had been called to the scene. The building had been stripped of all valuables, but there was no evidence, not a fingerprint. It was the perfect crime; the perfect mystery.

This continued for several months, break-in after break-in all over the world with no trace of the criminals. It started to get even stranger, buildings began disappearing, then people and soon the cities vanished. The world was slowly being taken until the day the stars went out and then the sun. The world became cold.

I was the last one that disappeared...

Jack Burt (13)

LAST NIGHT'S RECALL

Instantaneously I find myself in an alley surrounded by bodies, human bodies dripping with blood. Physically and mentally, I cannot comprehend what I am seeing. My mind is swarmed with questions. *How did I get here? What or who killed these people?* So many questions but so few answers. Beneath me, a glimmering object catches my eye and I pick it up. It's a knife. Suddenly, a swarm of flashbacks come flooding into my mind, bringing me back into reality. As I wonder who or what killed these people, it finally hits me. My questions are answered. I did it.

James Duncan (16)

JUST DESERTS

The autopsy had concluded that the victim had died due to blunt force trauma; a single blow to the head from a falling object. Death had been pretty much instantaneous. Detective Ignis Avem glanced around the scene for any missed clues. Foul play wasn't certain, but the problem was that a bloodied knife had been discovered and there was no sign of cuts or stabs on the victim. That was when Avem had decided to push some furniture around, discovering a crawl space. Inside, a beaten, cut, cold body lay. A double death, Avem concluded, but perhaps just one victim.

Louise Berry (15)

BRIDE-TO-BE

"We know you're here. Come out with your hands up."
Dance gracefully into custody? Lithe hands to the gods:
surrendering? I breathe, so tempted to chuckle.
I squeeze her limp hand, receiving her gratitude for the
crimson dress. It suits her groom. They shall be at the venue
now.
Once the men abandon modesty, they will dare breach a
lady's privacy of the folding screen and find a bride with
cold feet. Or perhaps they shan't if that's referring to myself.
The shutters are open, and the wind's not one to stop me. I
am off to my wedding.

Katie Winrow

THE MYSTERY: MISSING BOYS

Every night boys went missing from the hostel and no one could figure out where they were going.

Then Detective Corross came along and enquired. One night he found a man suspiciously walking in the compound of the hostel who looked like he was the culprit so the detective arrested him and everyone was relaxed now as he had been caught.

But then that very night another boy went missing from the hostel so they realised that the mysterious person they'd caught was not the person who was making the boys disappear. Then everyone was scared. Who would be next?

Shaun Augustin (11)

THE AWKWARD WHEEL

1,142 days I'd been here, each day being the same as any other. But this day was different. I had been wandering around and something caught my noise. Rotting flesh and decayed debris infiltrated my nose. Fighting the urge to inhale, I frantically scanned my surroundings in order to locate the perpetrator. Out of nowhere, a Ferris wheel came into view. This must have been forgotten. Curiously, I strolled towards it. I decided to jump on to see if it would work. It sprung into life! The ear-piercing music played as it went. Until it stopped. I was left hanging...

Josiah Edada

PAYDAY

Crack, the guard's neck went. Hoxton threw the corpse, concealed in a body bag, into the dumpster. Meanwhile, Wolf opened the security room door, took out the guard and disabled the cameras. The Harvest and Trustee Bank was ready to be swept clean. Dallas ran in with the thermal drill and placed it next to the vault.
Ten minutes later, it was open. The three of them stuffed their pockets and the duffel bags with stacks of money. They then threw their bags into the van. One, two, three. They jumped into the seats and drove away with £100,000.

Wilson Bartlett (12)

#8

"We're ready for the briefing."

"Our unsub is in his late 20s. We know he's well built as he'd need the might and solidity to murder those victims in such a brutal way. This unsub blends in with society, which suggests he presents himself in a way that is unthreatening to others. He uses a screwdriver and hammer as his weapon which tells us that he works in some type of maintenance job.

This unsub feels like an outcast, he feels betrayed by those in his past life. It is critical we catch him before he spirals out of control."

Osasere Edo-Jegede (15)

DOUBLE-CROSS

The sniper squinted his eyes. The crosshairs zeroed on his target. He counted the seconds in his head. One... two... chaos erupted. His target staggered, a patch of red appearing on his white shirt. His bodyguards scurried around him, catching his limp body as the life drained away from it. The barking of orders ensued as men in black began to pan out, searching for the cause of their leader's death. The sniper looked on from his spot on the roof. Slowly he turned away, frost creeping into his heart as he exited the scene of his best friend's death.

Ayesha Siddika

DARK WATERS

Her face twisted into a sneer as she stalked towards him. "You should be more careful. The world's a dangerous place."

He stumbled backwards until he hit the wall and realised how right she was: he really shouldn't have been senseless enough to go for a walk after the city's curfew. Maybe then he wouldn't be stuck in this stupid situation.

Like a snake, she lashed out, seizing his throat. Her nails were digging in and his vision was blurring but what chilled him most were her words. "You and me are going to have lots of fun."

Olivia Brockway (16)

THE LAST BREATH

Rachel's hands, icy cold and legs so frail she could hardly stand. She gagged from her own body odour. The babbling of the malnourished became constant and she tuned them out. Her skin was riddled with bug bites, her teeth loosened from lack of nourishment, and her lips craved water.
Rachel's crime was being Jewish, and the suffering had only begun. She didn't know where the train was going but knew it was bad.
In the last minutes of her life, when she and the others breathed in the noxious gas in the dark enclosed chamber, she adhered to hope.

Mirvat Anshur (13)

THE VICTIM'S BEST FRIEND

Everyone was shocked when Jessie Harold went on trial for a double murder. Bonnie Jackson and her older sister Haley were all found dead in their house on the night of January 21st, their parents still missing. Jessie Harold was a kind, gentle person and Bonnie's best friend. She was the most distraught when Bonnie and her sibling were found dead. She must have been a good actor because only one week after the news of the Jacksons' deaths, Jessie was taken into custody...

I knew Jessie was nice. After all, she's being convicted of my crime.

Ellie Lynch (14)

THE WHISTLE

It was a regular Saturday afternoon. Joey walked into the living room and said, "Mum, I'm going to watch a movie!" "Okay goodbye, Joey," she replied and left the house.

Joey stared at the TV and sighed. It was very small and slow. He sat down and found a horror movie called The Whistle; he loved a scare.

The car pulled up outside and it was 12 o'clock. He looked out the window and saw his mum on the ground, then heard a whistle.

Before being taken by the police he was last seen with a whistle in his mouth...

Gurveer Singh Matha (12)

THE DEAD SCREAMS

Aria was alone. She had no help. The wind gushed behind her. She stumbled through the derelict forest. The light dimmed. The night grew bitter. She needed help, but who? Aria stood still, trying to make out the blurry light she saw in the distance. She cautiously walked towards it. It was a house. She started to have hope.

Facing her fears, she knocked. No response. The door opened. Debating to barge in or not, she went and walked towards the light.

An ominous shadow lurked in the distance. A piercing scream went for miles. Aria was dead...

Saffron Ruddock (12)

SUSPECTED

Trepidation. It was all that I could feel - other than the shivers crawling down my spine. I would never have expected this day to come; I would never have expected to be here. Furthermore, I felt terrible anguish in my stomach as they asked me to stand up, their glaring eyes staring right through me.

As I walked into the room, he started asking me masses of questions. How were you connected to the victim? What is your name? Who are you?

Unnervingly, I opened my dry mouth to speak - nothing. And yet again, a great affliction lingered throughout.

Lana Force (12)

MIRRORS

Mother told me, "Never trust a mirror. Trust your eyes."
Sulphurous yellow fog hung inside the room. Grief made the
air thick and heavy. My candle drowned in wax as its flames
licked at my skin. The mirror steamed up, yet I saw a figure. I
gasped, looking back. There was nothing.
I turned to the mirror. Foul gloom blossomed amid the cold
air that hit my skin. I looked back again, my back facing the
mirror. Something grasped at me from behind. I shrieked,
looking back to see my reflection glaring at me and blood
oozing out my shoulders.

Kenusha Kalithasan

THE MURDEROUS SOMRAT

It was a dark night when the town of Shadowbury echoed with screams. Hundreds of heads lay cut off, blood everywhere.

The last time the town had seen this was when the Somrat was on the rampage.

Was the Somrat back? Why was this happening? Who created this ghostly creature?

The next day the town was swarming with detectives and bags as more body parts, feet, tongues and legs, were being found in drains, microwaves, bins.

Everyone was living in fear.

How long until this town was wiped out by this murderous Somrat?

So many questions, yet no answers...

Abigail Smithers (16)

DEAD?

Disappeared. Missing. Thought deceased. A funeral was conducted. There was no body to bury. Kara Jones was pronounced dead one chilly November morning, a young girl with a bright future ripped from her. Nobody forgot her.

A crack. A breach in security. Nobody knew who or why, but they were gone. In and out. No evidence, just an innocent photo, no clue as to what or where it came from.

An analysed picture. An audio clue. A frantic drive, a missing girl. Kara Jones was found one cold January evening, in a dilapidated house, standing over a dead kidnapper.

Lavanya Basu (14)

THE TOUCH OF AN ASSASSIN

"I saw blood. I saw the blinding glint of the blade of a knife. I saw... darkness."

I opened my eyes to regular light. I heard the screeching wheels of a trolley on a track bumpy as the back of a camel. I felt myself swiftly moved into a blue room. There were white hazmat suits holding long and thin tools.

The pressure of a hand covered my head and a panting voice whispered, "Everything will be okay."

My brain was rushing with a plethora of thoughts, *what had happened...?* All of which faded away into oblivion.

Oliver Johns

GUILTY INNOCENCE

"Charlotte Dickenson, she's guilty." Roy points a long, bony finger in my direction.

Sweat tickles my palms and I can feel my cheeks burn up. I run out of the courtroom. I must find out who did this if it's the last thing I do. I have been framed; I am utterly, completely innocent.

I stop at the glasshouse, this is where the murder happened. If I can find clues, my name will be cleared. I search and search until the big, juicy moon lights the liquid sky. A fingerprint. Wait, my fingerprint! This case is officially unsolved.

Evie Cassie

THE HEIST

Deep in the centre of London four thieves gathered outside Coutts Bank. Their names were: Jack, Alacey, Thomas and Tilly and they started to throw rocks at the box that was full of wires attached to the security system. They kept throwing rocks at the box until it and the wires broke.

With the security system destroyed, Thomas and Jack busted down the door and got a keycard from behind one of the counters and opened the vault. In total there was £8,000,000 stolen.

After that, they went in the Euro tunnel but we never saw them come out.

Alfie White (12)

SURVIVING ISN'T ALWAYS GOOD

I'm a survivor. I was the only one who was left alive that day. I remember the bodies... the blood dripping from them, the sound of people dying. Talking to the detective about it, they said, "You're the only survivor."
"Only me? Why?"
I remember the guy being dragged out by the police laughing. He was proud of the people he killed. I never knew why he did it until today. I wish I could tell you why he did it but I can't... If you're reading this I'm sorry for what I did but I didn't have a choice.

Millie Purcell (15)

DOUBLE CROSSED

Mr Harland Granger was found dead at the town square, with only few at the scene of the crime.

As the days passed more and more clues were slowly revealed with the help of my assistants, Jake and Heather. As I was going through the paper documents and clues, I linked all the information together and all clues were adding up to one answer - we had spies. Luckily, I had a suspect. Heather. But it was obvious she worked for someone, the murderer.

All our valuable information was stolen. We would have to leave this case... unsolved... for now...

Maryam Muhammad

THE GHOST

The Ghost. The most infamous criminal in all of history. All of the world's countries wanted them dead, but they never succeeded. Until now, when I found the first clue. The Ghost never left any fingerprints, like a ghost, but they always left random objects. In their latest robbery, I had found a can of soda. It didn't look special but that was when I spotted a clue, the can said 'made in the UK'. The Ghost's previous robbery had been stealing a nuclear bomb from America, not the UK. We finally had a clue to where The Ghost was...

Irtaza Nayab (12)

MISSING

The street was desolate, bins left out on the kerb, shutters barricading the outside world. A single piece of paper fluttered from a wall, damp and mangy with the steady drip of rain. It landed at my feet, swirling in a muddy puddle. The face imprinted on the dampening page had lost hope, only a shadow in a world of light.

One day she just disappeared, gone. Nothing but a memory. I bowed my head and carried on.

I arrived at dark; sobs rebounded on walls. I looked into her frightened face. She wouldn't be found. Not alive, anyway. Never.

Emily MacNaughtan (13)

THE INVESTIGATION

He stood there, shaken, unable to stop himself from staring at the ragged, slashed body of his father. Angry at who did this, he swore it to be his mission to find his father's killer. Thinking profusely, he surmised that it must've been someone who had a grudge against his father, his mind immediately racing to his mother, who his father had divorced. He remembered that his mother had a snobbish husband, but he hadn't seen his mother in a long time. He wasn't even sure if she even cared. But he knew he had to ask her about it.

Jacob Horrill

THE ENIGMA

It was a gloomy, sinister night. Anne was just coming back from her late-night shift at the hospital. She was driving her Lamborghini when she realised she was still ten miles from her abode.

"Got a long ride ahead," Anne uttered. What she didn't know is that this would be her last ride.

As she exited onto a one-way road, a furtive car waited in the shadows. As the car saw lights nearing, he turned on his engine and raced towards her.

The last thing Anne saw was a bright light. The last thing she heard was screaming...

Amina Conde

THE BLOCK STREET MURDERS

Just another day on the job, or so I thought, as I stood over the latest victim of whom we believe was the latest death in the case of which we now call the Block Street Murders. But as I examined the now rotting corpse, I noticed a letter hanging precariously out of the victim's pocket. Finally, a development in the case!

But as I retrieved the letter, I felt a cold rush of fear. The contents of the note read 'Hello Gilligan West' and '429 Block Street'. Anguish and fear covered me, for that was my name, and address.

Beth Rayner (13)

MY SISTER MARY

It's been three years since the disappearance of her. She was thirty-five nautical miles off the coast of Rhode Island. Only 15. She hadn't even experienced life yet. Not like the police cared. They would always say she will come back but no, of course, she didn't. You would think she would return nauseous and scared. Never did, never will.

I had planned to find her but mother said no. She said she didn't want to lose me too. I was only 13 but determined she would come back. Just one day she would be lucky enough to find home.

Millie Edwards (11)

YOUR SUCCESS IS MY SUCCESS

Blood pounds against my head and tears that I tried to hold in finally fall. "Ian... y-you know I didn't commit that murder, right? You-!"

"Oh, sweet big brother, I know, I know." He spares me all but a sinister smirk."Because it was I who killed that family. But it's like you said. Your success is my success, so I say, my failure is your failure, too, hmm?"

I see. All I can do is chuckle, maybe it was a way to get through the unbelievable pain jumping at my chest because this is what brothers are for, right?

Nnediogo Okezie (12)

DETECTIVE

I approached the yellow police line tape and ducked under it. A man in a blue uniform rushed towards me.
"Detective, the man was another victim of the same murderer from the last two cases," he gasped.
I nodded gravely as I approached the area. A body covered in white fabric was being removed.
Something caught my eye. A gold ring lying on the mud near the body had gone unnoticed. I picked it up and slid it onto my finger. That was too close. I watched the other police buzz around. They never suspected it was me all along.

Aleena Zaman (15)

■■■■ ■ ■▀■■ ■▀▀■ ▀▀ ■

Ever since I'd learnt morse code I hadn't been able to sleep. I was reading a book about the very topic when it happened. I was emersed in it, racing through with my newfound ability, feeling very proud of myself. Then my attention was caught by the pitter-patter of the rain just outside my window.

I looked out longingly, remembering the times I would sing and dance in the rain when nothing mattered but then. That would never happen again. What I heard was not what I expected. The rain kept telling me that if I dozed off I'd die.

Jessica Martin (15)

CURSED PREY

A delayed reaction time cried out in terror as unsteady floors swept away papers that smirked at their own evidence. Trails of blood circulated areas they had already walked past as they followed clues that were none but their own. Whomsoever knew the secrets of the darkness was cursed. A doll sat staring out of the window watching the rain as her cracked voice spilled out, "You are to suffer the same fate." Flashes of light lit up the room as thunder clapped. Another detective had come seeking a predator, not knowing he was the prey...

Hana Kawal (17)

FRAMED

Innocent or guilty? That question filled my head constantly as I sat in court. The suspect's face filled with streams of tears; every day he would claim he was innocent.

It was a dark, haunted night. I strolled home, tired and exhausted from the long day of tears and drama. Then a scream from a man flooded my ears.

I ran down the alleyway to find a body lying dead. I turned around. The suspect was behind me. He'd just come off the phone to the police.

"It's not nice to be framed, is it?" He killed that man...

Gracie Brindley (12)

HONG KONG

It was the year 1975 and a heist had just gone down. Hong Kong was lit up like a nightclub. The police cars were just howling around Hong Kong as they raced after the criminal that was getting away in a Ford Mondeo.

Bang. The car had smashed into four parked cars. Flames had ripped down the street like a dragon was present.

The man ran but didn't get far after being shot by three police officers right in the back. Dead. The criminal was finished. Turns out the criminal had taken out two sorry citizens in the police chase.

Kieran Davis (16)

I PROMISE

I did something bad.
They said I did something bad?
I don't understand.
They're looking for me?
The clock is ticking now.
That's what they said.
Tick-tock. Tick.
Stop.
It was a game.
Please, I promise it was a game.
Believe me.
I have to play the game.
Play the game.
Left or right?
Wrong or right?
The time is running out.
How could I forget?
Play the game.
How was I supposed to know she would...?
They'll find me.
They'll find me?
They didn't last time.
Play the game.
Play the game.

I was at home.
I promise.

Ruby Barry (15)

MR SIMON TAYLOR: EXPERT SCIENTIST

I analysed the sticky substance found on the road. So far no result had come to light but I was determined. My eyes faced the word 'unknown' numerous times. But one dark night, DNA was discovered. I found the match easily and we were soon to bust them.

As we made our way along the road, equipped and ready, we examined the case. A man had broken into a jewellery store and stolen fourteen watches and eight bracelets. He surrendered and I was promoted. Mr Simon Taylor finally meant something and I got the respect (and pay) I deserved.

Abi Fewings (11)

THE ULTIMATE CRIME

I throw my keys on the living room table and shout for my mom, who's always upstairs reading her 'How to solve a crime' book. "Mom!'' I exclaim in a loud voice.

While waiting for a response, I take a look in the sink to find the usual dishes that are there every evening. I spot a drop of deep red liquid that's too gooey to be water - I don't take much notice.

I still haven't gotten a response from my mom; I go upstairs. I start sobbing when I see her. I realise that this crime, she cannot solve...

Andreia Vasilean (12)

MOST WANTED RUNAWAY MURDERER

Last Saturday two guys went to the pub and played darts. One guy started mocking the other on how bad his throws were. The guy lost his temper. He grabbed him and dragged him down the side alley. He stabbed him violently. Blood spurted like a waterfall of rubies. He was dead.

The murderer ran but was seen by a witness. She called 999 and when they arrived they looked for evidence, found the knife and scanned for fingerprints. No fingerprints! The witness had taken a photo, but it showed no one!

Who is this ghost? The hunt starts now!

Nathan Hilton (13)

NO ESCAPE

People say to me that being a detective must be challenging. The drive you get to bring justice for someone is nothing that you'd understand. Unless you're a detective of course, but I'm not so sure about that.

This case was like no other. I looked down at the body, the only fault was the extremely pale skin, and I knew right away what had happened. It seemed impossible, yet it wasn't.

You think you're safe; I know you killed her. I will get to you, even through the pages of this book, and closing it is no escape.

Maisie Shea (15)

THE BLUE HAIR RIBBON

I was five, lying in my little bed staring at the small ballerinas my father painted on the ceiling. One night my window was left open, welcoming an unwanted visitor who strangled me with my own blue hair ribbon I wore every day to school. Their face and distinctive features still visit me in my dreams.

My spirit lives on in this house and new people were moving in today. I loomed down the steep staircase to catch a glimpse of the family I'd haunt next. There he was, my murderer with his upturned lip and scarred cheek. Mystery solved.

Isabella Trewhella (15)

STUART'S KILLING OF PC ROBERT

"Guilty!"

After five days in court, Stuart was found guilty of killing PC Robert. As he was led away from court he had flashbacks of the crime he'd committed.

Stuart broke into a house but somebody saw him enter so they called the police and Robert arrived. He entered the house and discovered Stuart thieving so he went to arrest him, but it was too late because Stuart had shot him. He died!

Stuart tried to run away but before he could the police found him at the airport and took him and the guns away. Stuart was given life.

Demi-Jo Smithers (12)

THE LADY IN RED

I never thought that would be the day that my boys would never see their mother again. I regret that morning, we had a fight about Harry and William. Diana ran out of the palace crying; I'm kicking myself I didn't apologise sooner. Harry and William rushed out to say bye to her, but I stopped them. I will forever live in guilt because they will never see her again.

The car crash that killed her was tragic. I couldn't help but think it was murder; my family didn't like her anyway. I'll always live in guilt. I am sorry.

Riya Kale

THE GETAWAY

I paced as quick as possible. All my teammates were getting impatient, so was my boss. I reached my destination. I ascertained that everyone was in the meeting room. The plan was on the table. I was expected to approve of it. Of course, there were a few changes but they were unnecessary. Then it was time to strike...

We got in the van and drove swiftly to the bank. We unchained the vent and climbed into the vault. All our strength and weapons were used. The shimmer of the gold blinded our eyes. This all happened without getting caught...

Amelia Atkin (11)

CHANGE

"People change," my mother recited to me on the car ride back from school.

I'd been bullied, again. These people never failed to ruin my education. I spent every day wishing I was somewhere else, like I was constantly on the wrong side of a gun.

But things are different now; it used to be them who teased me, it used to be them who made my life a living hell. But not anymore, I'm in control now. Now I'm stood here, the right end of the gun, waiting to pull the trigger. I guess mother was right, people change.

Ruby Blackbeard (13)

THE ULTIMATE CORRUPTION

Impossible! is my first thought as I find the massacred body. I was so careful when I dismembered the arms, neck, all parts that contain necessary DNA to identify a body. The bolt cutters gone, knife cleaned, how is the body not decayed? Now what to do? Yet again I'm drowning in blood. I must dissolve the body in acid, crush the bones. I was too weak to do this before but now I am not.
Bang!
I'm lying next to my victim, bleeding out! I knew being a corrupt officer would kill me. Can my murder ever be solved?

Mahiya Mohan (12)

THE BOY ON THE THRESHOLD

Lifeless on the ground, drowning in a pool of blood, all with a smile. The boy on the threshold had fallen. However, it wasn't as it seemed. The towering building watched the swarms of police cars and oceans of suspects. At the time of the incident, there was a party; anyone could've been a suspect. Was the boy a member of this party? Why would he jump? Was my suspicion correct? Many questions ran marathons in my small head, but all of them could be answered! A trail of red... A deadly trail. My legs had already begun stalking it.

Maria Sibi

I CANNOT SAY

I saw it all. The red paint splashed against the wall; the bleak grin of pure evil staring its victim in the eye as it shot him again. This time no screams.

I was engraved in my own mind, unable to confess what I had seen. The scintillating scourge of sentimental silence; not a word escaped the crimson pillows of my lips. I remembered the victim's cries, his face as death debilitated him, and the soulless murderer, no remorse, no mercy. Sentenced to an eternity in chains, I felt an innocent's pain. I saw it all, but I cannot say.

Iyioluwa Olagbegi

CRUSHED HEART

Walking around barefooted, Veronica felt the sand between her feet. With no food or water in her system, she felt dead. She walked around Verona Beach, helpless, as she saw no one around.

Suddenly Veronica heard a noise in the background. She turned around as she saw piles of dead bodies. Veronica turned back around as she saw a cult all wearing red clothes. They looked like people she knew, but they were dead!

Someone tapped her from behind, ripped her heart out and crushed it in their hands as she fell straight to the ground.

Elena Akumu

ON THE RUN

On the run. A thorough summary of my life. Starting off on a runaway train... and the end... I could sense it was close - very close. They were screaming at me to stop. To think. But never had I in my life ever done any of those things.
I kept on running. I guess it's true that your life flashes before you during your last moments. My life flashed past, like an infinite film. A jigsaw puzzle that hadn't been completed. A pen without its ink. It had been useless, incomplete. I tripped and fell, and then everything went black.

Akzhayaa Nimaleswaran (12)

A FICTIONAL MURDER

The many tales of Sherlock Holmes and Dr Watson had enhanced me as a child, reading by torchlight holding a notepad in my hands, trying out my own theories of what could have happened. I moved onto Agatha Christie novels as I grew older, spending hours trying to work out who to pinpoint the murder on. But despite my knowledge of mystery novels and the countless number of fictional murders I had managed to solve, I had never expected to be stuck right in the middle of a real-life murder. Especially a murder where I was the main suspect...

Katie Riley (14)

BILL THE KILLER

Three men were in a sky-high building on sky-high swings and *bang*... One of the swings got broken. This left the two men in shock about what they should do. The two men ran off but didn't call the police.

The body was found. They looked around the scene and all that was left was a hat with the name Bill inside. The police found lots of clues leading to where Bill could possibly be. "Open up," a police officer shouted. No response, so they went in and found the other two men hung up, dead. Killed by Bill?

Dawson D'Agostino (13)

THE END OF MY TIME IN PRISON

Prison's cold and dusty. As I walk down the line of cells I think about that night, that night I got framed... My cell is cell number 12 right next to the guard's quarters.

It's 5am roll call. As I climb out of my cell, I am confronted with the fuming face of a guard. "Get a move on, Beach." I don't like people shouting at me. My anger is taking over. *Bang!*

...Next thing I know there is a guard on the floor and blood on my knuckles. I know this is the end, then a gunshot. *Bang!*

Charlie Beach (12)

THE MASKED KILLER

People think that the dead can't talk; I thought this until I looked over the dismembered body. It was an average hot, sunny day in London city centre until I got the dreaded call from the crime scene investigator...
"Another body's been found."
I got there as soon as I could. When I arrived I took one quick look at the body; it had been beaten. It was bruised and taken apart, and of course, the same as the other murders, there was a mask lying next to the body covered in blood. It then clicked who did this.

Chloe Bridle (16)

THE CAR

It was a cold, stormy night with the forest trees dancing forcefully on the spot. A small road split the forest in two, and there were only two souls on the road. There was a man, a reporter driving blissfully listening to the radio when he came across it. There was a car parked on the side of the road that had a sort of eerie atmosphere around it. The reporter got out his car, crept over to the other and looked in the driver's side.
Screaming, he fell into the road. "This isn't right!" There was a headless body!

Rhys Teesdale (14)

WHO ELSE?

Something is missing but I can't see it. There's something I'm missing but what could it be? Perhaps I overlooked the evidence. No, that's not it. Maybe there were prints on the weapon, but there aren't any. It's impossible, there was no way out of the room. It was locked from the inside, unless... Yes, that could be it! The room that led nowhere, a hiding place, but for who? Wait, him? There is no way, right? But it has to be. There is no one else it could be. Why though? Unless the motive was. Damn, it was...

Tracy Owusu (16)

WHAT NOW?

Scrambling my knife into the dirty ground, I looked up to see hundreds of shining eyes staring at me. Jumping up, the wind screeched at me as I sprinted for my life into the darkness of the unruly night. Their flashlights stabbed my back as they scrambled after me; their voices pierced my ears, and their bright green vests glistened like the holy ghost who had punished me for my sins.

Looking back, I noticed some had stopped. Did I leave anything behind? Did I hide the knife well enough? The rest of them started gaining up. What now?

Olivia Beardsmore (15)

PSYCHO PIGS

On a gloomy morning, I decided to go to the lake. Every rooster needs to wash. Unexpectedly, I saw Gavin the goat lying there in the middle of the path. To my horror, he was impaled by a long sharp fork. I was mortified.

As I was searching for the culprit, I overheard their cunning plan, those psychotic pigs. It's senseless murder.

I ran to tell the others but it was too late. My brother Sebastian was dead! His cold face was unrecognisable. I ran with Greta the chicken to escape.

Will we make it? I can only hope...

Drew Marshall (13)

THE DEADLY CASE!

People think the dead can't talk! What if they could?
There had just been a very severe kidnapping involving a towering man who had kidnapped a seven-year-old boy in broad daylight. No one knew where the boy had been taken or why, but if someone had known, why would they keep it a secret?
As I am working with the FBI, we had to search the residence of the child. Why couldn't we find anything? Why was there no trace? Why was there no DNA? Or why was his mother not saying anything regardless of her son? Did she know?

Megan Guest (11)

YOU'RE NEXT

I got home from a long day at work to see her lifeless body lying on the living room floor. We were best friends. There were so many questions running through my head but I was more focused on finding out who did this to her. Luckily I didn't have to search for too long. On the kitchen counter there was a note. The note read 'I know you're wondering who did this. Turn around.'

As I turned around cautiously, I saw a man. Blank expression on his face, short brown hair. He looked at me. "You're next."

Charlotte Sayer (13)

BROTHERLY LOVE

It was a dark, stormy night and I had just finished work; tired, my bed was calling me. Retrieving the dirty key from my pocket, I mindlessly shoved it into the lock. *Click.*
I stepped inside and felt a chill run up my spine. Something didn't feel right. I thought the tiredness was getting to me until I heard the creak and heavy breathing somewhere to my left. Glancing in the mirror, I saw the glint of a knife. I spun around and felt it enter my chest. My last thoughts - *why would my brother do this to me?*

Alfie Ellson-Guidon (12)

COLD

Detective Abby stepped past the police line. The winter air brushing her coat was calming, almost like a fairy tale, but she had no time to enjoy it. She had to solve a crime.
She stepped inside. The smell of dried blood and maggots filled the air as she walked past the dust-covered halls. She followed the bloodied footprints into an open room. A young girl, with several wounds in the upper chest, lay dead on the floor of the main canteen. The detective slid her gloves on. She bent down near the body. Time to solve this crime.

Jessica Barucha (13)

THE AFTERMATH

You never realise what you've become until you become it. Standing over his body, his glass shattered on the floor. His eyes, his nose, his mouth, oozing black. Covered. Looking at his face, the poison in his bloodstream. His veins run like rivers of oil, twisting and pulsing. Poison is a wonderful thing. It can leave no trace, can be quick or agonisingly slow. For him, only the latter would be sufficient.
My first kill. Father would be proud of me. I can see it in his lifeless eyes and I can hear it on his blackened lips.

Jess Windram (13)

THE MAZE

1,142 days I've been here, trapped, all alone. Every day knowing that I'm going to be here in a never-ending maze. No exit. No entrance. Nothing. It is painful being stuck, constantly in a huge loop. Seeing the same things every day that I'm here. I'm hungry. I haven't eaten in days. I miss my family. I was kidnapped and taken far away from home, far, far away. I am a 13-year-old girl named Karen, I was bullied in school so I guess it's a benefit that I'm here. It was my dumb name! Wait! What's that?

Brandon Lewis

CORRUPTED TRACES

As the detective of the group, I felt something was off. What it was I couldn't quite pinpoint. They were hiding something from me. If I wanted to get anywhere, I had to find out. Everyone was sceptical. I had yet to find out who robbed this person's mansion, but there was nothing. No tracks, no traces. Everything was oddly clean considering they had no maid and hated cleaning. All signs were gone. But in being a detective for years, I knew a robber would never clean their tracks in time. Someone was stopping me. But who?

Sofia Bennett (13)

DARK STEPS

The room was filled with darkness... There was a flash of lightning... I rapidly looked back over my shoulder, screaming so loudly that your ears would bleed horribly... A person in a long black hooded cape was standing with a knife that was touching my back very gently.

Feeling petrified, I sprinted down the creepy hallway into a safer room. I saw a flash of purple. It was him running past the room... I heard his footsteps. I felt terrified as he came back. He turned the doorknob... He caught me... It was game over or was it...?

Ruby Doe-Stovell (13)

MISSING

There was once this man who had three kids and a wife. They lived a happy life, but one day the oldest child went missing. She never returned home after school. She was only 10. What could have happened?

The parents got really worried so they decided to call the police. The police came to their house and tried to help but couldn't do much because they didn't have much evidence to find the little girl. So they decided to give up and leave it as an unsolved case!

Everyone was getting worried. What should they do?

Emily Stevens (13)

THE WORLD IS BLIND

The world is blind - yet our eyes are open. We cannot see in the dark. We are blind - our reality obscure.

His eyes reflect hours of numbers, letters - more rabbit holes that lead to more questions. The answers hidden by the shadow of power.

Missing people forever cast in the oubliettes of history. Events never to be spoken of in the prime of their darkness. Makes you wonder what's behind the great facade of lies. He does wonder but the longer one lurks the faster one is engulfed by the shadow. He sleeps with his eyes open.

Arthur Jacquemin (13)

A GUILTY MAN'S DOWNFALL

A dying gasp of the arcane man as he flung himself to the floor like a caged animal. So quick he did this, the judge didn't have the chance to say guilty before the sickly suspect wrapped his thin hands around his wrinkled throat, and so swiftly that he was already on the floor before anybody could blink. All the officers ran to him and pulled his hands relentlessly, to no avail. No living thing saw the gallons of blood and carved dagger piercing the man's chest. How could this have happened? Who did this? Nobody knew.

Ellie Buckley

THE ONE THAT GOT AWAY

He drove down the street at high speeds, closely followed by me. The criminal had thrown himself through the window of a car and stolen it. He didn't know that the police were on his tail.

I wasn't a normal cop, more undercover. I was hurtling towards him from behind until he wound down the window and thrust out a gun. *Bang!*

I woke up in a hospital bed with pain in my head. There were three people gathered around me. I sat up in my bed as everyone walked towards me. What happened? Did they get away?

James Hall (12)

DEATH FROM A BROKEN HEART

My heart stops. Sudden. Violent. The blood from my veins seeps onto cold concrete. I want to scream but my lungs have no air. You did this. I trusted you with my everything and you did this. It hurts. It all hurts. My breathing is ragged... pained.

You are walking away. The knife glimmers with my blood. The lamplight. It is too bright for me. Your silhouette moves away as my eyes close. The darkness is a relief. My heart stops. Sudden. Violent. And a single tear rolls down my cheek. You did this, my love, you killed me.

Isabella Warburton Brown (16)

THE CONFESSION

I'd just finished school and was sitting in the park waiting for my friends when I noticed something sticking out of the bottom of a swing seat. I pulled it out of the seat. It was a piece of neatly folded paper. On one side was written 'Open me'. I was curious so I checked nobody was around and began to read. The note was a confession to multiple horrendous murders that had happened in our local area. I suddenly felt I was not alone when I saw a dark figure emerge from a gloomy corner in the park...

Lydie Solomon (12)

FRAMED

The sirens were deafening. I was resisting but the knot tying me down was too strong. The people who captured me talked for a while, but then they untied me and then tied themselves down as their van ran out of fuel. It was only at this moment I realised what was happening.
I could hear footsteps from the police outside the van. I quickly tried to find a way to make myself look innocent, but then they opened the door. I looked at the multiple guns pointed towards me.
I've been framed. What am I supposed to do?

Joshua Robb (12)

SING HAPPY BIRTHDAY TWICE

My hands were steady in the sink as the water slowly changed from a bright red to a softer pink. I turned off the tap when I thought I'd managed to get it all but realised some had managed to infiltrate my, now severely chipped, white fake nails. Turning the tap on again, and grabbing my switchblade from my back pocket, I picked at the dry red blotches with its tip. I dried my hands and looked into the cracked mirror. The expression staring back at me took me by surprise. A wide grin was plastered over my bruised face.

Rani Jadfa (16)

YOU ARE WHAT YOU EAT

My knife glinted in the midnight glow, and a frosty breeze crept through my window. A warm glow emitted from my candles, easing my eyes. My latest catch lay in front of me, a particularly large one may I say. Its head had already been removed, so it was less of a mess than usual. Scanning the lifeless carcass, I pinpointed the location to cut. I grasped my knife at the ready. It was the leg, where most of the meat lay. The knife pierced into skin. I grinned. I knew my customers wouldn't be able to tell the difference.

Koray Rogers (13)

THE ROCKS

Trudging through the forest, I spotted a large rock formation in the distance. It was only for a second, however, as the fog was turning as thick as a brick wall. I began to run as I could hear the movements of the creature in the distance. Edging closer to the rocks, I leapt into a small crevice that had been made from small stones falling.
I attempted to call for help, but it had centred me to the middle of nowhere. After a minute, I couldn't see it anywhere but felt breathing down my neck.
I was found.

Jack Archer

THE LATE-NIGHT ENCOUNTER

People think the dead can't talk but they can. It all came true when a detective took a late-night walk through a graveyard and heard a voice. It just didn't add up. Where was this voice coming from? He had to listen further.
He shone his torch where he thought he heard the noise. Hidden amongst the graves he saw a body move. A hand reached out to pass him a note dripping with blood. He read the note, being careful not to get blood on his hand. The note read 'under this grave lies an injured body'.

Dean Wilson (14)

THEY SEE ME

I hate the dark. Well, that's the same for everyone, I guess. It's in human nature to be so. Fear of the unknown is healthy, I think they say.

But I hate the dark in a different way. I hate the shadows it brings out with it. Every time, I see them. Their eyes, devoid of life, dripping with the tar-black blood of my guilt. Their hands gnarl and twist to point at me. They are blaming.

"I didn't want to do it!" I scream. My words echo in the hollow black of the cell.

I hate the dark.

Joshua Jogy

CRYSTAL CLEAR

It was like the blood rushing through me would burst out any moment. It was like my blood was boiling and would never cool down. It was like a part of me had woken. It was too much to handle.

'It' was called pain.

I remember the night crystal clearly. The heavy shovel in my hand, the dirt covering my body, the jet-black sky. I kept saying to myself - "What have I done? Why have I done this? How I am here?"

I was uncertain, yet so clear. I knew exactly why, when and how I had gotten here.

Coral Joseph

THE FAMILY BREAK-IN!

On an icy night, there was a mother and her teenager and a young daughter in the house playing family games. Until they hear a big thud and shatter... So the mum and young 15-year-old gentlemen jumped up as the young daughter was hiding under the dining table. As they were all panicking, the son discovered there was a break-in, it was a man all in black with a mask on so they had no identity. Therefore, they rang the police but as they did the mysterious man ran and attacked the young gentlemen... What will happen?

Rhianna Baker

GUILT...

In my bed I lie each night, eyes open. She watches me, I can sense her presence. Every day I sit in my cobweb-ridden, stained armchair, she is there... watching my every move. The murder was my biggest mistake. Even if I do confess she will follow. She is in my nightmares, my dreams... everywhere.
I remember the moment I stabbed her I was angry, I was furious.
I feel cursed, helpless. Tears drip down my face. No one to go to. Guilt gets the better of me. *Bang!*
...Dead in the moonlight.

Mia Wright (12)

THE SPIRIT SPEAKS

Hello, friends. Today I'm going to tell you about the day I died. I was alone walking home from a party and I was admiring the gorgeous lake. I loved the stars' reflection. Until someone pushed me in. I didn't see their face. Darkness. I saw darkness. Fear filled my body until my spirit left.

Yes, I am a ghost. I visit the police station every day to check on their progress in catching my murderer. It's been twelve years and they are not even close. Meanwhile, others like me have suffered.

Sofia Terry (14)

IT HAUNTS ME!

Guilty! Since I murdered her I lie in my stone-cold bed. I toss and turn. Nightmares! They come every night, fill my head with visions of her at the moment I killed her. I just got so angry. My murder is my biggest regret.

I walk down the street and she is there watching my every move. Her terrified face won't get out of my head and I hate it.

Her murder is still unsolved. It has only been a month. However, for me, it feels like years. I can't live with this. It keeps building up inside me.

Ebony Elliot (12)

MY DAD?

There was a flash of yellow lights as a deep engine roared past. Then a *sssccccrrreeeeccchhh* behind me. As if out of nowhere the dark grey BMW that was in front of me made a sharp U-turn and simultaneously flicked on its blue and red lights. Next, the sirens blared out and it hurtled towards the car that had spun out off the road and hit a tree no more than six feet tall.
As the police got out of their car, I now recognised the car that had crashed. It was my dad's car. But why was it here?

Charlie Godfrey (12)

THE GUNWARF MURDERS

The suspect was gone before I got there. All that was there was an empty car park and four neatly placed bodies in the corner, with bullet holes in the centre of their chests.
I looked around sharply looking for clues. In the corner of my eye, I saw a bullet shell in the crack of the multi-storey car park, hidden blatantly, like the killer wanted me to find it. I kept looking, and suddenly I saw a faint trail of some kind of sauce. I knew it was from Nando's. I rushed up there but I was too late.

Lucas Elwall (16)

A DOCTOR'S WORST NIGHTMARE

There was someone behind me... I didn't know who, but they were frozen in place. I turned round to see a police officer, but not any ordinary officer, this one thought I was the good guy, the one here to help.

The next day, the air was bitter and the atmosphere was more tense than usual.

I headed to the hospital like any other day and not even an hour in to work I had a patient in critical condition. As soon as I laid eyes on him I couldn't believe he found the same body and police officer.

Joe Silverlock (16)

MYSTERY

As I peered closer, I discovered that this wasn't an ordinary man. He was bigger than normal men.
As he placed the crystal on the ground, *bang!* I was thrown back and so was this man but not off his feet, unlike me. A force threw me against the hard ground.
He had heard me, and it was clear that he didn't like it at all... He came sprinting towards me and I managed to dodge him only by rolling on the ground.
It was a terrible idea to go and visit him! What did I need now?

Maysaa El Aoussi Hamdoun (11)

ON THE RUN

As I walked at a decently quick pace down the darkened, night-filled street with only lampposts to lighten my path, my mind started to drift to why I did it. Could it have been how it sounded so easy to escape the authorities and to do the thing itself? Or was it that I was growing bored, desperate, or something else?

No one knows what it is like to be on the run, to not be able to trust anyone or anything. Every person I go past I feel suspicious of. Every car I hear, *is that the police?*

Dexter Kitto (14)

YOU

It just did not add up. How could I be there at the time of the murder but not know how it happened? I only knew that I wasn't the culprit, but why was I locked in this cell? So many questions.
A security guard entered to give me my food, but there was something familiar about this guard. He was about to leave until I had the urge to stop him. Something was not right. When he turned around, he wore a sinister smirk on his face; all the memories rushed back.
I think we both know what happened.

Thalia Andrew

THE KIDNAPPING

I had an alibi; my brother told the judge I was at the gym. She didn't believe him. But the CCTV footage proved her wrong.

The three teenagers described the kidnapper as the memory flowed back to me. I was an actor until they ruined my job. The star of the show to a street rat.

I tied them to a chair. I was holding a gun to them. The memory will haunt me forever.

As the judge was about to let me go, a man came in and shouted, "I was at the gym that night with his brother!"

Finlay Borrett (12)

TALES OF JJ

One day, JJ went to visit a house that his father left him in his will. JJ went in the house and then found a little door that took him to the hidden room downstairs and he found the letter. He read it and it told him to go to a field.

So JJ went to the location and then found another letter that said to go to his father's favourite place ever. So he went to the park and found another letter saying, 'Look behind you' and his father was standing there saying, "I'm alive!"

Osian Roberts

THROUGH THE WINDOW

I stared at the unfinished piece of work that lay upon my desk. As I turned my attention to the clock, I realised I had been doing the same equation for the past hour.

Tired, I turned to my bedroom window which displayed a decent view into one of the neighbour's windows. I could manage to make out a woman holding a strange object. Averting my eyes, I saw a man stood in front of her. Hearing a bang, I saw the man fall onto the floor.

I sat on the edge of my seat, pondering on what to do.

Aleksandra Brucka (14)

GUNSHOT

It was 3am, I was sat on my sofa talking to my boyfriend. I was thirsty so I headed to the kitchen to get some water. Before I got into the kitchen I saw a dark shadow at the door.

I quickly closed the windows and my curtains and locked both doors, running into the living room. I heard tapping on the living room door so I blocked it shut.

I rang my boyfriend back to tell him what was happening but I heard a gunshot, then he said, "I'm sorry. I love you. He knows your address."

Sofia Mulliner (14)

THE MISSING PUPPY

I came home from work expecting to see my lovely new puppy waiting for me at the door, but when I got there he was gone. I searched around frantically but I couldn't find him. I grabbed my phone and called the police.

When they arrived, they searched the house and when they went outside they found him lying on his side, sleeping under a bush in my back hedge.

I apologised to the police and thanked them for coming here and helping and I spent the rest of the day with my new puppy.

Sebastian Winter (13)

THE GUEST ROOM

I showed Uncle Matt into the guest room and apologised - the lights weren't working for some reason. I watched him put his clothes away and noticed something strange on the wall. It was a painting of fields and a face bang in the middle. I could feel its eyes boring into me.

The next morning, I went to fetch Uncle Matt for breakfast. He wasn't inside the room. I looked around. Once. Twice. And then I realised something. There never had been a painting. It had been a window all along.

Kayra Saffet (11)

LITTLE CHOICE

Why had I done it? No, I had no choice... right? What started as flashes soon seemed reality. Blood on the walls, a bursting sound by my ear, bodies wherever my eyes drifted, a sharp pain, a hand across my throat, the screams and cries of the innocent - a screeching sound preached my nightmare. The world was spinning, only slight, for I still was able to make out the stones on which names of the past lay. I was in a graveyard, a figure of little height on the floor lay next to me. Dead.

Rosie Fitch (11)

GUILTY

The judge stared down at me, peering from above his desk as if he had the power from God. He looked, shook his head and banged his hammer on what looked like a coaster. Guilty.

The security, who was too incompetent to be police, put cuffs around my hands and led me to my cell so I could wait for the military men to take me there.

I cupped the bars of the cell with rough hands. Then I smiled. I knew what I must do.

I picked up the pillow and wrapped it around my head. Then I died.

Sahra Abdi (13)

UNWANTED COMPANY

It was a stormy night. Lightning danced across the sky. Thunder shook the earth and a ferocious wind pounded at a tin shelter where a glistening diamond once lay...
Meanwhile, the sound of police sirens flooded the city of London. A dangerous criminal was on the loose! And she was heading for the vault!
Darting out of the way of the bustling crowds, the thief continued on her way, thinking only of the riches that lay ahead. Little did she know, she had company...

Katie Assad (11)

THE BOX

It was his 9th birthday today. No one knows what he looked like or what happened to him but I do. You see, I have never seen his mother before until today. She hides herself in a little shack a few acres away from my home. It's quite desolate there, creepy too.
I went to visit my ma and that's when I saw her dig out a box. It had the initials 'JC' on it. I saw the bones. It looked fragile, small and weak... It only took one guess to know whose it was.

Jiya Goldy

TRAPPED

I was stuck in here for 28 days, yes, I counted. My legs feel numb and my arms... my arms. I can't feel them anymore. Every single second I'm in the same position. Legs crossed, all squished up in a cage just waiting for food and energy. What's the point of life if I can't socialise, learn or have fun? I should've told him to kill me straight away. How dumb was I to think that the police would find me in this old, haunted house?

Wiktoria Grzesica

THEY'RE COMING

The sirens began to boom: the hunt was on. I watched the others leap into the lake. None of them surfaced. As I waited for a sign of life, I looked behind me. *Crunch! Crunch! Swoosh!* Something was behind me but could it be? My legs began to shake profusely. I began to run into the darkness. The others were likely to be taken and I didn't look back. I heard another siren in the background. They were coming!

Nicholas Ridgway

THE HAUNTING CRIME

It's been two years since I murdered Mrs Murphy. I still feel like her blood is on my hands. I can still feel the fog curling softly around my ankles. I remember her screams of pain. I remember the moment I stuffed her in the ground.
I don't really come out anymore. I stay within my abode. If people knock, I pretend I'm not home.

Edward Thompson

YOUNG WRITERS INFORMATION

We hope you have enjoyed reading this book – and that you will continue to in the coming years.

If you're a young writer who enjoys reading and creative writing, or the parent of an enthusiastic poet or story writer, visit our website **www.youngwriters.co.uk/subscribe** to join the World of Young Writers and receive news, competitions, writing challenges, tips, articles and giveaways! There is lots to keep budding writers motivated to write!

If you would like to order further copies of this book, or any of our other titles, then please give us a call or order via your online account.

Young Writers
Remus House
Coltsfoot Drive
Peterborough
PE2 9BF
(01733) 890066
info@youngwriters.co.uk

Join in the conversation!
Tips, news, giveaways and much more!

 YoungWritersUK @YoungWritersCW YoungWritersCW